# The Joy of Gluten-Free

A Practical Guide to Live Gluten-Free and Thrive

AMANDA SILVER

NEWMAN SPRINGS PUBLISHING
320 Broad Street
Red Bank, NJ 07701

First originally published by Newman Springs Publishing 2020

Verses taken from the Ryrie Study Bible New International Version,
Ryrie, Charles Caldwell, Moody Publishers, Chicago, 1994.

Cover photo taken by Angela Hale
Family photos on page 24 taken by Karen Light
Tamarind Seafood Soup photo on page 96 taken by Anna Himelstein
Ethan's Smashburger photo on page 150 taken by Ethan Silver
Almond Cake with DF "Butter Cream" Icing photo on page 176 taken by Anna Himelstein
About the Author photo on page 200 taken by Whitney Witzczak
All other photos taken by Amanda Silver

ISBN 978-1-64801-747-6 (Paperback)
ISBN 978-1-64801-763-6 (Hardcover)
ISBN 978-1-64801-748-3 (Digital)

Printed in the United States of America

To RoseMary
1939–2018

# Acknowledgment

I gratefully acknowledge our Lord and Savior Jesus, apart from whom I can do nothing. I am thankful for my godly hard-working parents for their sound example of good values. I thank my mom for her excellent proofreading, Katrina Nichols for getting me started, and my dear gluten-free family for always telling me the truth about the food and how they feel. I appreciate Steve's patience with me as I have often been more of a mad scientist than a wife, and both the kids are my heroes for not only sticking to it, but also taking this whole new life seriously creating their own fantastic foods. I thank our doctors, Dr. Joseph Childs, Dr. Charles Durr, and Dr. Lance Lipton for bringing us all back to excellent health and for all the teaching that they naturally conveyed.

All along the way I had many encouragers for whom I am intensely grateful: Angela Blair, Kesha Hearn, Jean Diver, Trish Davidson, Whitney Witczak, Jackie Dragoni, Cheryl Payn, Angeliea Carson, Francine Covelli, Diane duPont, Jake and Donna duPont, Christine duPont, Jen Stemple, Sina Ebnesjjad, Grace Engbring, Dr. Susan Epps, Prudence Fenton, Mary Garrett, Angela Hale, Lizzie Hoag, Roger Crain, Sarah Light, John and Karen Light, Rachel May, Jamie Magee, Darcie Ward, Mahnaz Yousefzadeh, and especially my RoseMary, RoseMary Kinsey.

# Contents

Prologue ................................................................................................................ 13

## Section 1

Chapter 1
    The Facts of Life Concerning Gluten ................................................. 19
Chapter 2
    Our Story ............................................................................................. 25
Chapter 3
    Before You Start .................................................................................. 31
    I) What Is Your Why? ......................................................................... 31
    II) Expensive? What is Your Life Worth? ......................................... 32
    III) The Best Test .................................................................................. 32
    IV) What's the Story with Leaky Gut? .............................................. 33
    V) The Elimination Diet ..................................................................... 35
    VI) When Should I Start? .................................................................... 37

## Section 2

Chapter 4
    The Battle Plan .................................................................................... 41
    I) Mind-Set: Prepare Your Mind ....................................................... 41
    II) Prepare Your Kitchen ..................................................................... 43
    III) Standing Firm ................................................................................ 49

## Section 3

Chapter 5

The Approach to Food ...................................................................... 53

I) Looking Ahead ................................................................................ 53

II) Leftovers? Sounds Like a Bad Word! ........................................ 54

III) Organic? ....................................................................................... 56

IV) How in the World Can I Possibly Make this Work? .............. 57

Chapter 6

Meal Planning and Shopping: Planning Ahead............................ 58

Chapter 7

Gluten-Free Living with the Children ........................................... 61

I) Reflections of Ourselves ............................................................... 61

II) Gluten-Free in Public—the Questions to Ask........................ 63

III) What to Do about Lunches! ...................................................... 67

IV) Snacks and Treats ........................................................................ 69

V) School Birthday Celebrations ..................................................... 69

Chapter 8

Traveling Wisely and More Eating Out ......................................... 71

General Notes on Cooking................................................................ 72

Bone Broth and Rendered Animal Fats......................................... 79

How to Cook Vegetables .................................................................. 83

Broccoli, Cauliflower, String Beans, and Zucchini or Yellow Squash.... 83

Beets ................................................................................................... 84

Brussels Sprouts................................................................................. 85

Roasted Vegetables ........................................................................... 85

Spinach Three Ways .......................................................................... 87

Mushrooms ........................................................................................ 88

Soups

Potato Leek Soup .............................................................................. 91

Butternut Squash and Bean Soup ................................................... 93

Onion Soup ....................................................................................... 94

Cod Fish Soup with Mustard and Singapore Seasoning .............. 94

Tamarind Seafood Soup ............................................................................... 97

Sides, Salads, and Snacks

Sautéed Baby Kale ...................................................................................... 101

Rosemary Roasted Sweet Potatoes .............................................................. 102

Roasted Green Tomatoes ............................................................................ 105

Curried Collards and Potatoes .................................................................... 105

Latkes ........................................................................................................ 106

Apple Sauce ............................................................................................... 107

Homemade Stuffing .................................................................................... 108

Korean-Style Noodles ................................................................................ 111

Lotus Root Kinpo ....................................................................................... 112

Salmon Egg Salad ...................................................................................... 113

Shrimp and Avocado Salad ......................................................................... 114

Chicken-Artichoke Salad ............................................................................ 114

Chicken Salad ............................................................................................ 115

Italian Tomato Salad .................................................................................. 117

Tomato and Cucumber Salad ...................................................................... 117

Cucumber Salad ......................................................................................... 118

Asian Salad ................................................................................................ 118

Israeli Cabbage Salad ................................................................................. 119

Quinoa Salad ............................................................................................. 121

Pasta Salad with Black Beans ..................................................................... 121

Puglia-Inspired Pasta .................................................................................. 122

Roasted Pecans ......................................................................................... 123

Chewy Fruit and Nut Bonbons .................................................................. 125

Spinach-Artichoke Dip............................................................................... 126

Dressings, Sauces, and Seasoning Mixes

Traditional French Vinaigrette.................................................................... 129

Mustard Vinaigrette ................................................................................... 129

Sherry Vinaigrette ...................................................................................... 129

Sesame Dressing ........................................................................................ 129

Tamari Ginger Sauce .................................................................................. 129

Mediterranean Dipping Sauce .................................................................... 130

Spicy Thai Peanut Salad Dressing...............................................130

Barbecue Sauce.............................................................................130

Fruited Balsamic Vinegar.............................................................131

Hamburger Seasoning...................................................................132

Lamb Seasoning............................................................................132

Creole Seasoning..........................................................................132

Main Courses

Meats and Poultry........................................................................135

Roast Pork Butt or Shoulder (Fresh Ham).................................137

Steak..............................................................................................137

Pork Chops....................................................................................138

Lamb Chops..................................................................................139

Lamb Pops.....................................................................................139

Leg of Lamb..................................................................................140

Crispy Roasted Whole Chicken...................................................143

Roast Duck....................................................................................144

Steak Chili.....................................................................................147

Hamburger Stew...........................................................................148

Lambites or Lamburgers...............................................................149

Smashburgers.................................................................................151

Italian Turkey Meatballs...............................................................151

Lasagna..........................................................................................153

Mediterranean Spaghetti Squash.................................................156

Shepherd's Pie...............................................................................157

New England Crab Cakes.............................................................159

Simple Salmon Bake.....................................................................160

Beautiful Grouper (or Orange Roughy or Tilapia).....................161

Main Course Sauces

"Cream" Sauce with Peas and Ham.............................................165

DF Spinach-Artichoke Sauce.......................................................166

Desserts

Brownies or Chocolate in Fives...................................................169

Angel Food Cake..........................................................................171

Chocolate Chip Pumpkin Cookies ........................................................................ 175

Almond Cake ...................................................................................................... 177

DF "Butter Cream" Icing ................................................................................... 179

Banana Bars ........................................................................................................ 179

Chocolate-Chip Banana Squares ....................................................................... 180

Blueberry Cake .................................................................................................... 183

Pumpkin or Squash Puddings ............................................................................ 184

      Pumpkin Pudding ........................................................................................ 187

      Dairy-Free Pumpkin Pudding OR Egg-Free Pumpkin Mousse .................... 188

Quick Almond Olive Oil Cake ........................................................................... 189

Almond Thumbprint Cookies ............................................................................ 191

Blueberry Pie ...................................................................................................... 191

Bibliography ........................................................................................................ 193

# Prologue

So you've just found out the "bad" news that you are gluten intolerant. You feel you may never enjoy your food again because so much will be missing. Your family and friends look upon you with pity or horror—or worse—with ridicule because they do not believe in gluten intolerance. Chinese restaurant owners' eyes glaze over, and they practically walk away when you come to see what you could possibly eat there. Yes, it happened to me! Dear reader, I know this sounds awful but I implore you to keep reading because there is great hope and happiness ahead for you and your family.

To add to this mountain, you may even have found out that there are other things besides gluten which one or more family members must avoid most, if not *all*, of the time. The idea that you must now cook for all your loved ones—essentially be the warden of your family's new jail, keeping them from eating the wrong things—carries at once an overwhelming sense of dread and duty. But I am getting ahead of myself. This is how you might be feeling if you actually *know*.

Maybe you have had the celiac disease test, which came back negative, but you continue with a variety of symptoms. Your doctor may be at a loss to come to any definitive diagnosis. Perhaps he or she keeps prescribing new drugs, which don't seem to help, the side effects of which require other drugs. As time goes on there may be new aches and pains or maybe a sudden onset of some chronic disease, neurological difficulties, or you may have a history of headaches. This is just a smattering of the possible maladies, which, surprisingly, are often directly related to the ingestion of gluten. As you will read below, in my family there were quite a few seemingly unrelated symptoms in each of us which all turned out to be due to gluten.

If you think you may be gluten or dairy intolerant you probably are. If you think that you are too old to change, I want you to know that it is *never* too late to have good effects and feel better from a gluten-free and possibly dairy-free life. Even at advanced ages people have made great strides in coming back to health from the debilitating effects of gluten. The following are some of the many ailments from which you could be suffering and which you even may have accepted as normal. This list, unfortunately, is only partial.

- headaches
- stomachaches
- joint pain
- fatigue
- skin problems
- dental problems
- bloating and gas after eating
- constipation or diarrhea
- candida overgrowth
- AD spectrum symptoms
- neurological conditions such as brain fog, anxiety, or sudden emotional outbursts

### What is Functional Medicine?

The question of gluten intolerance is best diagnosed and answered by a doctor of functional medicine. These doctors look at the whole system of the body to find the root causes of illness and pain instead of just treating the symptoms. It is this type of doctor that you need to read the results of the best blood test and then draw up the proper course of action. I hope that you will seek out the functional doctors near you and soon get yourself and your family on the road to recovery.

This book about practical solutions and encouragement in the life adherent to the gluten-free and possibly dairy-free diet is not just a book of recipes, but more importantly, it is one to help to bring the reader into a new state of mind. We must take control of our own health, and since this has largely to do with what we feed ourselves, I believe that we have to begin with a positive attitude of determination in order for the decision to change the diet to stand. I have found that books on this subject, though they may be well-intentioned, thorough and good, they lack the true demonstration and practical solutions for family to live everyday life.

Whether you have settled this question of gluten intolerance or not, the truth is that if there gluten intolerance, there is a need for a practical approach, which takes into account your *emotional wellbeing* in order to see the change through and, even more so, in order to stay the course for life. It took a long time for this bad state to become bad enough to be noticed and so it will take some time to undo the awful effects of gluten in the body.

The strength and vitality gained from the gluten-free life also depends on the health of your digestive tract. I believe that people who earnestly go gluten-free often fail because they become discouraged and give it up before they have its good effects. The reason is usually that they have not healed the small intestine through a short-term anti-inflammatory diet (also called the elimination diet) and the regulation of the metabolism. This subject, the permeable gut, is even more important than the knowledge of gluten intolerance; and though there are many other causes of leaky gut, it very often leads back to gluten intolerance. Another reason that people who "go gluten-free" do not attain the healing that should happen is that they have not actually removed 100 percent of the gluten from their diets.

The gluten-free recipes included are clearly marked as to other problem foods they may contain such as dairy, eggs, nuts, or legumes (beans). I have also indicated elimination diet adjustments to exclude these ingredients wherever it is possible. I pray this will get you started and help guide you in your own new life.

When you look this problem square in the face, you must not run and hide; you must stand. Your family needs you. Yes, it was difficult to learn to feed everyone, but we have been managing for some years now and want to help others. You must now know that you can never go back to a casual or impulsive way of choosing to eat anything. However, the most wonderful thing is that, done right, the symptoms of the inflammation caused by the offending foods go away. Not only this, but also you will find new energy, courage, and even joy as you go forward in this new direction. I want you to know that you and your family can do it and even become a help to others. I have written this little book to help guide you and teach you good habits for your new life and encourage you in your journey to very good health.

# Section 1

# CHAPTER 1

# The Facts of Life Concerning Gluten

Send forth your light and your truth, let them guide me: let them bring
me to your holy mountain, to the place where you dwell.

—Psalm 43:3

This chapter is optional to read because I would rather that you receive the practical information and encouragement, the whole point of this book, than be bogged down with technical information. This chapter may be very interesting for some, but depressing or overwhelming to others.

## So Many Effects!

Gluten intolerance is so often thought of as a digestive issue but you might be surprised by all the systems in the body affected by gluten. This intolerance is an immune response, not an allergy. The way that gluten affects one depends on the genetic composition of the individual and where the weak link in his or her DNA lies[1]—the place where inflammation will occur.

Very early on in our new life (before I knew about my own gluten intolerance) I earnestly attended a three-hour talk at a hospital not far away given by a man named Dr. Tom O'Bryan. Having already set my hands to the task of feeding Steve and the kids without gluten, and having talked to my sister's friend with celiac disease occasionally over the years, I thought that I knew something about gluten. This doctor blew my mind about five times

---

[1] "The Gluten Conundrum," A speech given by Dr. Thomas O'Bryan, Paoli Hospital, Paoli, PA. April 27. 2012. Hereafter noted as O'Bryan, "Conundrum."

over. I was not prepared for the wealth of information and intensity of these few hours. I am utterly thankful for the result, which was and remains my resolve to take it all very seriously.

Tom O'Bryan, DC, CCN, DACBN is a teaching faculty member of the Institute of Functional Medicine, the National University of Health Sciences, the International & American Associations of Clinical Nutritionists (where he is a certified clinical nutritionist) just to name a few positions. He has made great strides in raising public awareness through his website, theDr.com (where you can see that these few sentences hardly do him justice) and broadening the knowledge of other health coaches and professionals teaching his Certified Gluten Practitioner course. He holds many diplomas and certifications making it his life's work to help people who suffer from gluten-related disorders which are underdiagnosed and, thus, undertreated, to heal through diet and nutrition. He founded and was the host of the Gluten Summit, theGlutenSummit.com (which was brilliant) in which he brought together twenty-nine experts across the world to contribute knowledge from each of their health modalities concerning gluten-related issues. Dr. O'Bryan, himself, is a highly passionate and engaging speaker, whom one should not miss, if given the opportunity to hear him.

One of the many things Dr. O'Bryan imparted to us that has always struck my sense of the truth was simply a slide of three brain scans. I could see that there was a dark area somewhere in the brain of each of these people, each with a neurological disorder. One was schizophrenic, one bipolar, and the third had anorexia nervosa. Dr. O'Bryan told us that each one was gluten intolerant. He taught us that gluten cuts off the blood flow to the brain.[2] There are many ways that gluten can affect the brain from these examples to ADHD, and the many disorders on that spectrum, to migraines or simply recurring headaches. All of which are serious.

Since every one of us has different DNA, there is a myriad of possibilities for the ways in which gluten can affect our organs and/or our systems for the worse. One example from my own experience of dis-ease directly caused by my eating of gluten is this: my *elevated liver enzymes* mysteriously found after the birth of our second child Ethan showed up again on my comprehensive blood panel nine years later. I had no idea that something was even happening to my liver. What would have happened if I had not stopped this?

The fact that I had to write down all the illnesses, aches, and neurological symptoms I have had in my whole life brought a lot home to me. It is *not* normal to be constipated from childhood often and get pneumonia and bronchitis in one's thirties along with a whole lot of sinus infections and other illnesses. The real shocker was the miscarriage just the year before, after which I came up with a ringing in my left ear, a terrible dizziness that would suddenly

---

[2]  O'Bryan, "Conundrum."

wake me up at night after I had been asleep only about twenty minutes, and I was also having a hard time thinking of the words I wanted to use while speaking. I could not believe all the stuff I was writing down. I even felt obliged to write down the knee pain I had had from the age of sixteen, which I had always attributed to not rehabilitating it well enough after having broken my leg. My knee pain has been gone ever since I quit gluten! During the Repairvite (elimination) diet I was given some supplements for my liver and in two months it was healed to normal functioning! Almost immediately I stopped being awakened by that scary dizzy feeling and have *never* had it since. With the neurological therapy I was receiving at our doctors' office, I could feel that my brain was healing and improving. That's the great thing about the brain—neuroplasticity! It can heal.

The gluten test given by medical doctors is often falsely negative because the person is only tested for celiac disease. Although it is more well-known, celiac disease (CD) accounts for a small group in the manifestation of gluten intolerance, which is evident as only one block of gluten proteins to which the body reacts. The person found to be negative may yet be intolerant of other gluten proteins *not* on the test.[3] Furthermore, celiac disease may be the most virulent and well-known form of gluten intolerance, yet its detection may also be missed because fifty percent of these patients do not present symptoms in the gut, but neurologically.[4] Because gluten crosses the blood-brain barrier, it is a major factor in the onset of a huge number of neurological disorders.

Non-celiac gluten sensitivity, or NCGS, is just as serious as celiac disease but has remained elusively difficult to diagnose. The excellent doctors who are painstakingly making these diagnoses must do it by ruling out celiac disease and wheat allergy. Another of the many great sources of information is Chris Kressor, MA, LAc, whose article, "3 Reasons Gluten Intolerance May Be More Serious than Celiac Disease," I ran across a couple of years ago. Before anyone with CD gets upset, I just want to say that it was simply bringing awareness to the fact that not only is CD terribly undiagnosed, but also NCGS is probably even more undiagnosed. The forum attached to it illustrates how incredibly serious all of it is and how varying the symptoms, experiences, and emotional reactions are concerning celiac disease and non-celiac gluten sensitivity. ChrisKressor.com is another excellent fount of information concerning these things with his facet of Paleo nutrition added to the mix of functional and integrative medicine.

Because all sensitivity to gluten causes the gut to be permeable, a myriad of problems can then ensue. This loosening or opening of the tight junctions between the epithelial cells, the first layer of cells inside the small intestine, allows the wrong things to get into

---

[3]  O'Bryan, "Conundrum."
[4]  Prof. Hadjivassiliou, Marios, MD, UK, *The Lancet Neurology, 2010 Mar.*

the bloodstream. These things include toxins, parasites, and food particles too large for the body to handle. Most toxins and parasites actually pass through the digestive system having little effect on the body in the healthy individual. The food particles are too large because the flora, or good bacteria, of the digestive system in the gluten intolerant person is compromised and also, fewer digestive enzymes are present so that the digestion process is hampered overall. It is these overly large food particles repeatedly getting into the bloodstream because of gut permeability, which eventually cause the body to become sensitive to any number of foods besides gluten.

Because 75–85 percent of the immune system is within the gut it follows that the gluten intolerant people who continue to eat gluten have a compromised immune system.

Because of the strain on the whole system through the ingestion of gluten, the weak link in any individual's DNA is then stressed.[5] Thus, gluten can be a major external factor which causes one's *proclivity* to cancer or autoimmune diseases, such as diabetes, thyroid disease, fibromyalgia, psoriasis, and Meniere's disease, to name a few, to *become the disease(s) in reality*.

In view of the incredible complexity of the digestive system in action as our immune system, I highly recommend a book *The Definitive Way to Go Gluten Free* by Joe Rignola, HHC, FDN to anyone who really wants to understand what is going on in the body. He writes in plain language and makes it quite entertaining (if only it were not such a horrific subject). In his clever banter he explains very well what is happening to the lining of the small intestine when gluten is introduced in either CD and NCGS creating zonulin, a protein that actually opens the tight junctions therein allowing said terrible things into the bloodstream. Rignola's book follows the research of one of the major leaders who happens to be the founder and Director of the Center for Celiac Research in Massachusetts, Alessio Fasano, MD. Fasano, discoverer of zonulin in 2000, a world-renowned pediatric gastroenterologist, has written *Gluten Freedom*, which really is, as it states on the cover, the "essential guide to a healthy gluten-free lifestyle," and so I would be remiss not to mention this book. It is his research to which O'Bryan was referring when he said, "No human on the planet can digest gluten, whether or not it causes symptoms" on one of his webinars.[6]

Just one more subject before I leave this unpleasant lecture. I am going to have to say something about GMOs and what they do. Genetically modified organisms or GM crops by their very nature are not only causing our good bacteria to be killed off but also contributing to leaky gut. Jeffrey Smith, the executive director of the Institute for Responsible Technology, writes, "a recent analysis of research suggests that Bt-toxin, glyphosate, and other compo-

[5] O'Bryan, "Conundrum."
[6] Dr. Tom O'Bryan, iTeleseminar.com/76603494.

nents of GMOs are linked to five conditions…Intestinal permeability, Imbalanced gut bacteria, Immune activation and allergies, Impaired digestion, Damage to the intestinal wall."[7] The Bt-toxin present in GM corn and GM cotton (both used to make widely used cooking oils) is a pesticide, which kills the insects by "punching holes" in their digestive systems. Just the year before this was written, a "study confirmed that it punctures holes in human cells as well."[8] Further, the glyphosate (main ingredient of Round-up) in Round-up Ready GM crops like soy and sugar beets is known as an herbicide but it is also a strong antibiotic, which "can significantly reduce the…beneficial bacteria and promote the overgrowth of harmful strains."[9] This is frightening combined with Judy Carmen's 2004 paper recounting how very little testing for food safety has been going on (and it continues as such today) by the very companies who make and sell these patented seeds and poisons.[10]

So really, as these facts gather and one begins to see the common thread of the problem of leaky gut, one is able to see that the avoidance of GMOs is of the utmost importance going forward to heal and remain healthy.

[7] Jeffrey Smith, "Are Genetically Modified Foods a Gut-Wrenching Combination?" http://responsibletechnology.org/glutenintroduction, Nov. 20, 2013. Hereafter noted as Smith.
[8] Smith.
[9] Smith.
[10] Carmen, Judy. "Is GM Food Safe to Eat?" Hindmarsh R, Lawrence G, editors. Recoding Nature Critical Perspectives on Genetic Engineering. Sydney: UNSW Press; 2004. P. 82–93.

*Amanda, Steve, Nina and Ethan, January 2006*

*Nina, Steve, Amanda and Ethan, September 2018*

# CHAPTER 2

# Our Story

Brothers, as an example of patience in the face of suffering, take the prophets
who spoke in the name of the Lord. As you know we consider blessed those
who have persevered. You have heard of Job's perseverance and have seen what
the Lord finally brought about. The Lord is full of compassion and mercy
—James 5:10–11

In my family, everyone is gluten intolerant. However, the way we found this out was quite involved. My husband had had back and neck pain, sciatic neuralgia and terrible psoriasis for many years, but suddenly of late, he also had a racing heartbeat at times, brain fog, fatigue, and bleeding gums. In the fall of 2011, Steve found a chiropractor's office that is doing things a bit differently than what is usually expected. As they are also functional medical practitioners specializing in neurology and metabolic blood work, they look for primary, secondary, and tertiary causes of pain, and then work to help the patient recover from these things. Steve was immediately sent for a comprehensive blood test and a separate gluten sensitivity test unlike the one commonly prescribed by a general practitioner.

As I have, in my own life, studied the effects that foods have on the body and information beyond the knowledge in the mainstream, I have been seriously considering becoming a certified gluten practitioner. This course is given by one of my favorite doctors and sources of knowledge of the effects of gluten on the body. I want to help others to learn and maintain the precepts of the gluten-free life in an official capacity—to be there for them to guide them in the process of making their diets safe and delicious.

However, as a mother's time is so precious and full, my education thus far has been the hands-on experience of feeding my family within the boundaries of a gluten-free diet, which includes other individual food sensitivities in our family.

I so wanted to write about the jams and jellies I have developed since 2007 while running my small business. Alas, in the midst of this venture at the end of 2011, there had been so many illnesses, conditions and disasters happening to all of us, culminating in the discovery in the first half of 2012 of the gluten intolerance in every one of us, that I had to take a step back. I have kept the business going but all the while have been cooking in a new way and educating myself (and the rest of us) about the important and mandatory changes in our whole lifestyle.

Instead of writing a book all about my original jam and jelly recipes, I find myself writing about all the terrible symptoms and conditions that our family have been through because I think it could benefit others if the story sounds familiar to them. It seems now as though we have been living this new gluten-free life forever. It was December 2011 that I had had to endure a D & E because the baby had no heartbeat two months into my pregnancy. That had been so heart breaking for Steve and me. I don't know how anyone else deals with the loss of a baby. I thank God for my close friends at church whose prayers and comfort I could not have done without. It did not seem connected, but it was at the same time that Steve was waiting for results of testing done with the new doctors he had found. In January 2012 he found out he was indeed gluten intolerant.

This was something I had suspected for several years leading up, and which I think he had also, but for a long time he would not go to a doctor to find out. I am sure he knew what it would mean, his favorite food being a ham and cheese on an Amoroso roll. Not only Steve's urgent and frequent bathroom stops (even right in the middle of Sunday dinners at his Italian-American mom's) through the years, but also, it seemed as though our beautiful children were sick so much more than their schoolmates.

Our first child, Nina, so bright and creative with her thoughtful and fun-loving sensibility began to have tummy-aches before she started preschool. Every now and then she would say her tummy hurt. It was usually around when she had gotten over a cold—or that was the question the pediatrician would ask. Then we were invariably told that discharge from the respiratory system going down into the stomach would easily upset it. We accepted this for quite a long time, as it was not every day that she mentioned it.

By the age of six, her tummy pains were more frequent and sometimes accompanied by headaches. She had reflux and she had to avoid acidic foods. This was seen by an X-ray while she was actually drinking a barium "milkshake". I kept a food diary for a month and she was no better on a "reflux" (reduced acid) diet. I cringe now as I read everything my little daughter ate, seeing that *so much* of it was gluten. A month later she was put on a well-known acid blocker. I gave it to her for almost three months (not fully the prescribed time period) and watched my child worsen each month. Because I did not know then what I know now I believe it was God that prompted me to start giving her probiotics the day I took her off the pharmaceutical. There was immediate marked improvement but the problem did not go away.

I read all kinds of information, went on GERD (acid reflux) websites, and talked with health food store personnel. I have many notes on a hundred pieces of paper to document her pains and what I did for her. One even has a direct quote from Nina at seven years old before breakfast.

"Oh, Mommy, I don't feel good at all. My stomach is hurting and it feels like I can't breathe. I have an awful taste in my mouth."

She seemed better after some food and I took her to school. I can't imagine how many days she must have felt so awful.

We had Nina back at the doctor at the age of nine when she was in so much pain and could not eat more than a bite at mealtimes for days. It was discovered by a different X-ray that she was completely blocked up. The following treatment was more terrible than ever. She had to have nine tablespoons of polyethylene glycol in thirty-two ounces of a sports drink (another gluten carrier) within two hours. For a while after that Nina seemed better and she had to continue the medicine daily at a much smaller dose, but the problem continued.

So now we were just about up to Steve's discovery of his gluten intolerance. That year, Steve's psoriasis (an autoimmune disorder) seemed to explode in concert with a case of poison ivy he got in the fall. Not only this, but he tells me that he was also experiencing difficulty in comprehending, say, an instruction manual, or motorcycle manual, which should have been second nature to him. He was reading the same sentence three times without understanding. He tells me that this brain fog was not the only adverse neurological effect going on, but also, periods of hot and cold sweats connected with feelings of anxiety. I may not have noticed this because I was busy getting excited about a third child. As I have already said, that was not to be.

As soon as Steve was found to be gluten intolerant early in 2012, we had the children tested because we were aware of the genetic aspect of this condition. What a relief it was to actually find that poor Nina, who had been wrongly diagnosed with acid reflux years before with struggles to remedy it to no avail, was gluten intolerant instead. In fact, her tummy aches were not due to an overabundance of acid, but instead a lack of enough acid to digest her food! It took the whole time between the age three and the age of ten to find the true cause.

I remember when Nina, just eleven years old, had already been avoiding gluten, dairy, and soy to heal her system; she would be able to reintroduce dairy and soy after about six weeks. At the time, our son, at the age of nine was also found to be gluten intolerant. I had already seen the emotional effects of this diet change in my daughter and I knew that nine-year-old Ethan needed to have a memory of the last day. He still remembers when I allowed him to have a sweetened cereal for breakfast and his dad took him out for a donut after school. Although this may seem like a very normal day to many people, we thought it was terrible that knowingly we allowed him so much gluten! But I also knew that we would never go back. This was the demarcation line. When the decision is made it should be forever and we have kept it so. We hardly ever look back because we are in such a different place.

The great thing is that when you consistently make this change it shows up in how you feel very quickly. Right away I noticed that the kids were less sickly (though they did not always like to admit it, knowing that it was this difficult diet change that made them feel better). Tummy aches and headaches were going away.

Funny and how human *I* am that I was the *last* to be tested not expecting the results at all. Steve said I had to do it too, and I agreed to be tested—just to rule it out, I said. Ha! I never even thought it would be me—and on top of that, I found out about additional sensitivities. I never thought that my extra high energy would be due to my inability to make my own GABA in my brain to calm me down because of the gluten. What?! I have neurological effects? I never knew that it was pounding on my liver—something in my DNA that was vulnerable to the unbreakable strings of protein that is gluten. These were the unknown things that would have continued and progressed toward my early systematic degeneration, if not my early death. I am ever grateful to know the truth!

There is much more to this way of life than just avoiding wheat, rye, and barley. There are often other food sensitivities in addition to this infamous group. My husband, Steve is also intolerant of casein, a protein in all animal milks and dairy products. He must avoid casein in the same way that we all must avoid anything with wheat, rye, or barley or any of their derivatives. This is because it is one of the things that are called cross-reactors. A casein molecule looks to his body just like a gluten molecule and, thus, causes him to make gluten antibodies as if he has had gluten.[11]

It is true that when there is gluten intolerance, there is often also the intolerance of casein. There is so much information on this subject that I leave it here just to make the point that, while all of us must never be contaminated with gluten, Steve is just as vulnerable to contamination by dairy. One can see why it is of utmost importance that, while the rest of us can still have dairy, his food be prepared with great care, uncontaminated with dairy. He is also sensitive to buckwheat (which is no relation to wheat) and millet and has, himself, decided to avoid them almost altogether.

The children and I all have a sensitivity to egg; our doctors tell us it must simply be limited to one or two times a week. Also, I have sensitivities to corn, potato, sorghum, and rice. These sensitivities, though less dire, are still important to observe.

---

[11] O'Bryan, "Conundrum."

There are conflicting opinions, but our doctors say that we should "cycle" these things so that our bodies can recover from the small amounts we have ingested.[12] This requires us to know *when* we have eaten these things. Therefore, I keep a small food calendar, just to quickly notate these things, so I know when the last time was that I have given the kids eggs and when I have eaten anything on my list of sensitivities. My aim is to try to stay about four days away from the last time. Unfortunately, the main flours used in commercial gluten-free baked goods are brown, white, or sweet rice flour, with other starches and sugars derived from rice, potato and corn used as well. I have had to resign myself to very little, if any, of these things.

Now I must tell you that I left off writing this book for almost a year. For some reason or changing reasons (and a few bad excuses) I could not sit down to finish. From October through December, I was consumed with the everyday chores and requirements to keep the growing children in school and jam in the shop, as Steve was very often gone visiting his father in the hospital. Sadly, his father passed away soon after Christmas. Ethan seemed to be sick often which raised in me suspicions that there might be something else going on. In early December it was confirmed that Ethan was now intolerant of casein and he had also become sensitive to rice and oats.

I must say that the boy, then twelve, took it all very well, accepting the new adjustments and avoidances in his diet while I was the one who cringed when I realized the next thing he could no longer eat. He told me that he didn't care, and it was worse when I would make that apologetic face, and would I please stop. I learned from my almost-thirteen-year-old how to act properly! He was right. There is no sense in moaning and crying over...

The reason I just wrote that immediately above, is that I want you to know that it is still possible to cause ourselves to come up with new sensitivities and intolerances. It was just before school had started when Ethan learned how to make his own grilled cheese sandwiches. I was truly thankful for this because now he could make himself another great snack (in addition to cooking eggs which I still needed to monitor as he still needed to be reminded when he last had them). And then Halloween happened bringing probably the greatest hoard of chocolate I have seen in my life. Nina did not go trick-or-treating anymore but Ethan had his crew. I saw it go up to his room and then in the next month I knew that he had been eating this chocolate at record speeds. Between the grilled cheese sandwiches, the many bowls of cereal and the Halloween candy he simply had too much dairy, too much rice, and too much oat. This shows that it is very important that we eat a varied and moderate diet! I now also believe that the GM ingredients in the national brands of chocolate (the milk and soy lecithin) played a part in this fiasco.

---

[12] From a private consultation with my doctor, Joseph Childs, DC, DACNB.

As you can see, dear reader, there are complications in feeding the average family that has various food sensitivities and intolerances. But if this is also your truth I want you to know that you are not alone. The things you will do for your family are important and far-reaching as you and they will not only regain the health and vitality a family should have, but will also learn the right path through life in the future.

# CHAPTER 3

# Before You Start

Test me, O Lord, and try me, examine my heart and my mind; for your
love is ever before me, and I walk continually in your truth.

—Psalm 26:2–3

## 1) What Is Your Why?

In view of the change that you are about to commence, it is vitally important to settle your
mind on the reason or reasons that will carry you and encourage you to stay the course. One
very important thing to know about gluten is that a relapse can possibly cause a much worse
reaction. So, if you already know you should not have it you must swear off it completely.
Above all, it is important to be tested *before* you change your diet. Otherwise it will not be a
true test because the antibodies will not be present in a meaningful way. It is also important
because when you see it in black and white you cannot deny it. Some people are *still* hard to
convince of the importance to stop, even after they know. Ask yourself: if you *know* a thing
is poison to you, would you really keep eating it?

The kind of food that I hope you will seek out not only fuels and strengthens your
body, but also supports the producers who are growing it in the most natural and life-sup-
porting, earth-enriching way. Whatever you may believe about the good stewardship of the
earth aside, you should ask yourself *why* you would do this. Consider what is of great importance to you and install it in your hard drive so that nothing can shake your resolve.

Every person is different. Do you have a history of cancer in your family? Diabetes?
Other autoimmune disorders? Arthritis? Osteoporosis? Are you tired of being tired or
fatigued? Have you ever felt a slowness or fog in your brain—the inability to find the words?
Do you want to be healthy and vital in the lives of your children and grandchildren as they
grow and discover the world? If you know or think that you are gluten and/or casein intoler-

ant and may possibly have other sensitivities, this new mind-set, and the life that it demands, is a valuable path to unmistakable change.

## II) Expensive? What is Your Life Worth?

You may have the notion that it will cost an outrageous amount. I hope you will seriously consider whether it is worth saving a little money now, only to be in and out of the hospital starting in your forties—or even earlier—with one or more chronic or autoimmune conditions or, I dare say, cancer, for the rest of your life, be it long or short. Or would you like to make the act of eating a purposeful and concerted effort to get the *best* that your money can buy which will heal you and give you energy for all the great things you want to do in your life?

It is my aim, not only to show you some recipes and suggestions on how to solve the problems which arise in a world full of gluten, but also to help you see that a completely new approach to preparing and eating food is necessary.

## III) The Best Test

Cyrex Labs
www.CyrexLabs.com
Tel. (602) 759-1245
Fax. (602) 759-8331
5040 N. 15th Avenue, Suite 107
Phoenix, AZ 85015

It is the very best thing to have the very best blood test. This is not, however, a recognized test by the FDA and, thus, is not covered by the insurance companies. Some doctors may consider gluten in the diagnosis of your mysterious symptoms and blithely prescribe an old test, which nowhere near does the job. Many false negatives are the cause of many poor souls who go away relieved that they do not have to change their diets, do continue to eat gluten and, of course, become even sicker. The very best test is done by Cyrex Labs. The results of this test must be read by a competent doctor of functional medicine. It is the most comprehensive rundown of many more gluten antibodies—not just the small group which indicate celiac disease (a small percentage of the many manifestations of gluten intolerance). Not only this, but also, this lab can test for what other sensitivities or intolerances you may have. Your stool should also be tested for any parasitic activity that may have occurred because of the leaky gut. Wait! What is that? Leaky gut? Read on food warriors, there is healing to be done before we settle on the life-long diet.

Leaky Gut

Oh, I know this sounds horrendous. It is. One of the many things that occur over the years, as a gluten intolerant person continues to eat gluten, is that he or she has the unfortunate reality that the small intestine becomes permeable. This allows toxins, large undigested food particles, and even parasites to pass through the intestinal wall into the bloodstream. Any one of these things can make us really sick. These food particles, from which the body/blood cannot receive the nutrition through the proper function of digestion, now become something like invaders, which the body rejects. This is one of the reasons that other food sensitivities are found when there is gluten intolerance. Contrary to some beliefs, there is really no relationship between these types of sensitivities—they happen when the body just decides it has had enough of whatever it is.[13] So if you eat a lot of something while your gut is permeable (like me with potatoes and rice) it is likely at some point you could become sensitive to it. While I was putting this book together much more information had come out about the serious implications of the leaky gut. As my husband reminds me often lately, it is most important to find out if one has leaky gut. This condition is caused by a myriad of environmental sources such as pesticides and antibiotics in our supposedly healthy foods, not to mention the over-prescription of antibiotics, plain old OTC pain medicines (called NSAIDS) and our own stress hormones.

## IV) What's the Story with Leaky Gut?

"Hold 'er Newt!"
(My grandmother always said that and I finally heard it in an old western.)

Please do *not* immediately run out and buy all the gluten-free bread, pasta, and snacks you lay eyes on. First we have to heal the gut. If you have already had the simple test (the one that *is* covered) and it has indicated your intolerance to gluten and you cannot get the better one, you *can* find out your other sensitivities through the *elimination diet. But also,* if you think that changing to a gluten-free lifestyle is done simply by exchanging one type of bread or pasta for another you will never get well.

Whether or not you care to find out any other of your food sensitivities, you need to go on this far stricter diet *to heal your gut* (your small intestine). It is a temporary time of one month to three in which you must avoid *all* inflammatory foods and sugars so that the metabolism can regulate and allow the healing of the lining of your small intestine to hap-

---

[13]  O'Bryan, "Conundrum."

pen. One of the main actions of this special period of time is that your metabolism will be stabilized without the sugar spikes and your body will stop creating stress hormones, which contribute to leaky gut.[14] This is another reason to get the Cyrex test because the functional doctor can see *how* permeable your gut has become and thus prescribe the *proper length of time* for this anti-inflammatory diet.

Vitamins and Supplements

Being under the doctor's care also will give him or her the opportunity to see in what you are nutritionally lacking because of how the gluten has affected you. At the same time as Steve and I were on our elimination diet we were given vitamin and herbal supplements and also a preparation of herbs and enzymes which aided in the process of healing our digestive systems. This preparation called RepairVite by Apex Energetics Nutritional Complexes was to be used in conjunction with the RepairVite diet protocol created by Datis Kharrazian. This protocol by which Steve and I healed our leaky gut, better-known in this book as the elimination diet, is the anti-inflammatory diet. There were also things prescribed to remove parasitic activity, and to clear signs of infection. Nina had some supplementation along with her lesser form of the diet. Because of her youth, the gluten had not had as much time to make her intestine as permeable as ours although it had hurt the balance in her digestion. A good *probiotic* is one of the most important supplements you should take every day because of the destruction of the beneficial flora in the gut caused by so many factors of everyday life not to mention the bad effect of gluten on the system. During the writing of this book I learned that, more importantly, we should be eating things known as *prebiotics* to feed our own good bacteria.

Well before this had been a subject in recent health news, Stephen Gundry, MD, FACS, FACC, wrote *Dr. Gundry's Diet Evolution*, which champions the care of the microbiome as the best path to losing weight. Probiotics are indispensable on the road to recovery but as his book states, we keep having to take them every day because they are not our own beneficial bacteria and thus, pass through. So as we go forward, the ingestion of prebiotics helps our own beneficial bacteria (starved into scarcity by our prior bad diet) to multiply and begin to work properly for us. I recommend his very interesting book for better and more information on this but for our immediate purposes I list here some prebiotic foods: garlic, all types of onions, mushrooms, asparagus, artichoke, peas, organic soybeans, jicama, dandelion greens, avocado.

---

[14] Explanation of reasons for elimination diet in a private consultation with my doctor, Joseph Childs, DC, DACNB.

One of the other very important supplements that all of us take is EFA DHA because essential fatty acids are so beneficial to the heart, brain, and the entire blood system. There are some others such as coenzyme CQ10 and NAC, but it is best that you consult your doctor for the things you need.[15]

The worst thing to do when you find out you are gluten intolerant is to go out and buy a whole lot of expensive baked goods (which will not taste good to you yet, anyway) and just substitute these in your regular diet. This can actually cause weight gain and, more importantly, with the permeable state of your gut, might even cause you to become sensitive to new foods your body has never seen before, or ever had in such quantities.

Now, that said, I am here to tell you that this will be one of the most empowering times of your life as you gain control over your cravings. You can do it! It is such a short time compared to the length of your whole life. You will probably start feeling better within two weeks—and if not, do not despair! Your comfort and vitality are just around the corner.

## V) The Elimination Diet

And the God of all grace,…after you have suffered a little while will
himself restore you and make you strong, firm, and steadfast.
—1 Peter 5:10

Oh yes, this diet *is* hard. But…you can do it because it matters! Remember that this is only temporary. With patience and intention you can get through this. Here is what you CAN eat:

- organic, pastured meats and poultry
- fish (preferably wild caught)

*I, however, seriously limit large fish such as tuna and swordfish because of dangerously high amounts of toxic heavy metals.*

- fresh vegetables (with some exceptions)
- leafy greens
- berries
- banana (1 or less per day)
- fruit (with a few exceptions)

---

[15] Recommendations of Dr. Joseph Childs and Dr. Charles Durr for patients in their practice.

- sweet potato (see sidebar rules for this and other starchy vegetables)
- extra virgin olive oil
- red or white wine vinegar
- apple cider vinegar
- coconut aminos
- herbs
- unsweetened coconut
- coconut oil
- unsweetened coconut milk

What you CANNOT eat:

- wheat, rye, barley, malt, or anything malted (and this is forever—including all derivatives named in my section on ingredients and labeling)
- all other grains (which includes rice, corn, cornmeal, cornstarch, and any other derivatives of grains)
- dairy products
- eggs
- legumes (beans, and that includes string beans, peas, and soy, which includes tofu and soy sauce)
- nuts
- seeds (which includes tahini)
- nightshade vegetables (these are tomatoes, eggplant, and peppers—including hot sauce, cayenne, and paprika)
- mushrooms
- sugar, honey, maple syrup, agave, or any sugar substitute
- kiwi
- watermelon
- guava
- mango
- pineapple
- canned fruit
- raisins

## Ah! Sweet, Sweet Potatoes!

Thank God they are no relation to the potato! However, they do contain a lot of sugar. SO it is important, especially on the elimination diet, that you do not make a whole meal of a sweet potato. They can be eaten after some good protein and vegetables to keep your metabolism from spiking. The following rules also apply: no more than two servings per day, no more than 25 percent of any meal, and never on an empty stomach. These rules also apply to the other starchy vegetables, which are allowed: turnip, rutabaga, and parsnip.

- coffee
- chocolate
- alcoholic beverages

Hang in there! It will not be like this for long. How many times can you eat that big leafy green salad without tomato, cheese or nuts? Devise different ways to cut the cucumbers and carrots. Add shrimp or chicken. And after you have that salad you can enjoy the crunch of those delicious sweet potato chips. (The ones combined with beet chips are great, too.) When you are sick of roast chicken and turkey bacon for days on end and want to cheat with chocolate and ice cream, *don't do it and don't give up*!

The only way this will really work is if you go the full four weeks (or more) without all these things inflaming your poor gut. When you feel hungry and helpless because it will take too long to warm up that leftover steak or turkey, eat it cold. Or be more determined and find a way to warm it up.

One of the most important things about this whole diet is *not* to be hungry. Remember that we are trying to level out the metabolism, so it is tantamount that you eat LOTS of little snacks of all the accepted foods. This is why it is so important to form a habit of packing fresh vegetables, fruit and beef jerky (if it is very simply made—and without nitrates and nitrites) to have with you wherever you go throughout the day. This habit will serve you well in your new life as you may not always have the choice of proper foods even when you are back to eating more foods. Not only will you heal your permeable gut, but in this process, you will also lose (or seriously curtail) your cravings for sugar!

This is just the beginning. Consider it boot camp because it *will* get easier, I promise. As a good friend often said to me "we are sharpening steel on steel!" You are going to feel better and better. This is so worth it, and if you give in and eat the wrong things you are going to have to start your day count all over again!

## VI) When Should I Start?

Considering when one might begin the elimination diet one might think about the time of year. It might be a great thing to do it in the summertime when the kids are out of school and there are plenty of fresh vegetables available. Some might consider the first of the year a good time to create new habits and maybe it's as good a time as any. I hope you don't put it off too long because the sooner you do it the sooner it will be out of the way for you. Even though we knew that Steve was intolerant early in 2012 he did not make the commitment to do the elimination diet until about March when I knew that I too was intolerant. We did it together so we had each other's support.

# Section 2

# CHAPTER 4

# The Battle Plan

## I) Mind-Set: Prepare Your Mind

*Do not conform any longer to the pattern of this world, but
be transformed by the renewing of your mind.*

—Romans 12:2

My whole reason for writing this book is to have you know deep down and unshakably that the journey on which you are starting is the best action you can take. First, you must prepare your mind to embrace this new way of living and eating. Although it may seem difficult to fathom the fact that, in the first stage of this new way, you are eliminating every type of inflammatory food from your diet, the real difficulty is in your long-term ability to *maintain* the comparatively easier course. This course will ultimately be the source of your vitality. It requires you to change the way that you think about food now and forever.

You may be feeling overwhelmed and depressed by the prospect of this whole new life, but I want you to begin this journey first in the mind with a few things about our food, which, to me, are far more overwhelming and depressing.

You may actually have heard that over the last half century there has been a great deal of change in the food supply. According to many sources in the last fifty years the gluten in the wheat has increased fifty times what it originally contained.

The crops most readily available, such as wheat, corn, and soy, are not the same as those on which our grandmothers or even our mothers grew up. Without delving too much here into what I think of GMOs (genetically modified organisms) I will say that I know that the companies who sell these seeds have not found out or will not publish (admit) the long-term effects of them on the human body.

There has been extensive testing in other countries (not accepted by the US FDA) and almost every other country has banned GM ingredients in their foods or these crops to be imported. This issue is important because the genes of these "foods" may soon be proven to cause changes in our own DNA, which may be yet another influence in the great increase in the instance of gluten intolerance and many other food allergies and sensitivities.[16] This is not even to mention the known poisoning of our fruits and vegetables with pesticides and herbicides, which cannot always be washed off, and the application of antibiotics to our produce of late contributing to the destruction of the good bacteria inside the digestive tract.

So the food supply has changed, but let us view truthfully the actual composition of the diet itself—the American diet. At the risk of sounding like your mother I might ask, are you eating your greens? How much sugar do you have every day? Unfortunately, the idea of meat and potatoes to many people translates to burgers and fries in as much time as it takes to drive around a building! We are constantly bombarded by advertising while we are hungry for lunch or late at night, bored,—well, at any time of the day, really. How is a person to resist all this temptation? We even (sadly) end up with a terrible acronym for the "Standard American Diet." Yes, it is SAD.

Consider the "food pyramid." Supposedly it has been improved in recent years, yet we are still to include a great deal of carbohydrates, which we are to ingest mostly as grain and try not to eat very much fat.[17] As a result of this decree, the instance of obesity, diabetes and autoimmune disease has increased in only the past few decades at an alarming rate sometimes referred to as epidemic! Thankfully, there are some excellent doctors who have shown how effective the good saturated fats are in the healing and working of the organs of the body, in particular our precious brain.[18] They have shown that, rather than what the common "healthy diet" dictates, a low carbohydrate diet with plenty of good fats causes weight loss. How could we have gotten so far away from reality?

Of late, having traveled outside my usual locale—to a big wedding, a women's conference large enough for an arena, and a funeral—I am compelled to write a few things that I had not expected to feel. I really realized the frequency of America's unhealth. I guess I was more oblivious than I thought to the truly widespread pain and dis-ease due to the state of our food supply. It is not always the incidence of obesity causing our unhealth but that even those that appear to remain within a "normal" weight range are experiencing one or more autoimmune conditions in a sea of abnormality.

---

[16] Smith.

[17] Davis, William, MD, *Lose the Wheat, Lose the Weight*, p. 59.

[18] Perlmutter, David, MD, *Grain Brain*, p.36.

Another problem I see is that people seem to accept their conditions quite naturally and think nothing of taking a pharmaceutical for whatever it is. Whether it is some neurological disorder from "mere" headaches to a psychiatric evaluation such as bipolar disorder or anxiety, there is no thought of trying to discover the cause. Another prominent diagnosis I keep running into is one of the disorders of the thyroid. The solution to which often seems to lead to the removal of that organ. Thus, that person must stay on thyroid medication for the rest of her life. The answer to such things as fibromyalgia, psoriatic arthritis and Crohn's disease seem to all be similar drugs with horrific side effects which, of course, pretty much disable the immune system.

Still more troubling is the blanket statement that the causes of these things are unknown. This is absolutely unacceptable to me since I have been reading so much material about so much research that shows there is a great connection between all these immune disorders and our food. This is research to be found in major medical journals, which are out there for all to read. It is sad that the doctors who seem to want to treat these things have no time to read this copious body of research in the last thirty years. I understand that they have many patients to attend to but it is my belief that doctors should allot time to read research. It seems very simple to me. I am a mother who cares for her family with food sensitivities and intolerances, but I am also able to read this research and understand it.

What is of utmost importance here is that you, dear reader, change your whole *mind-set* from convenient eating to eating to nourish the body back to vibrant health and to fuel it to keep the immune system working properly. You must not think of this as a diet from which you can take a vacation or on which you can cheat just a little. You will really get somewhere when you stop seeing food as your reward or way of celebration. But this does not mean there is nothing to enjoy! You are on the cutting edge! When you eat what is best for your body and avoid things of which you are intolerant, you give a lifelong gift to yourself and your family.

As you go forward you are going to not only shed the weight and discomfort caused by gluten and other food intolerances and sensitivities, but you will also be released from your addiction—yes addiction—to wheat![19]

## II) Prepare Your Kitchen

For I know the plans I have for you, declares the Lord, plans to prosper
you and not to harm you, plans to give you hope and a future.
—Jeremiah 29:11

---

[19]   Davis, William, MD, *Lose the Wheat, Lose the Weight*, p.52–54.

In this section you will learn how to transform your food storage and preparation areas into a safe and clean environment out of which you and your family's health and strength will be born. Despite the general ideas and complaints you may have heard, it is easier than you think. Here, again, the importance of your new vision concerning what is actually food and your intent to set yourself and your family apart from the mainstream belief system about food is of the highest order. Remember, again, that you are on the cutting edge! One day there will be loved ones who will turn to you as they have their own realization of what must be done. I know that you will be able to direct them with confidence because it is the truth.

I was speaking recently to a dear friend whom I know well and whom I know as a great cook. She knows my passion for this new life and how I feel that, among others, she and her family would benefit from being gluten-free. I often hold back, but I do sometimes entreat her to make the change. She has over time come around to considering it. Often she lets me know how, when she has control of the cooking, she does cook gluten-free and how the result is usually a calmer household.

This conversation with my girl, which follows, really illustrates the problems and thoughts of one who may be thinking about or who must begin the new way. She said she bought the books. I do not know which ones, but there are many good books written. The only thing is that I think many of the books are so informative and encyclopedic that they overwhelm. Knowing her, I am sure that she read a good deal and got the picture.

The next thing she said (expressively) was that she would have to replace all her cookware. At last she said she looked into the pantry and seeing there the massive job of removal and, of course, thinking about all those products no longer usable, she said, forget it!

My friend is not ready to make the change yet, but you, dear reader, are ready to embrace a new and healthy life for yourself and for your family. Part of the difficulty for my friend is that her husband will not listen to any of this and just wants to eat the things he always has. This, unfortunately, sends their son the message that these things are okay and are allowed. It illustrates another important point. If there is one (or more) in the household who are unwilling to eat your way you can still make the change. It all depends on your new empowered mind-set and good labeling!

Labeling pots and utensils for the adherent members of the household is good way to keep the sensitive ones safe. Even in our completely observant household we have a whole shelf in our fridge on which the dairy items go because it is easier to know right away which products are safe for my dairy-free husband and son. (Truth to tell, eventually I relegated all dairy products to the basement fridge and have been using less and less of them. It is a lot easier.) The best thing that my friend could do is simply have their son (actually, everyone) tested and there will be no more conflicting ideas. She is close to doing that.

Let us look again at her statement and let me put your mind at ease about some very important things. Yes, many of the things you have used in the past for cooking any foods with gluten will be off limits to you in your new life. However, this does not mean that you need to break the bank to help yourself.

The list that follows here is of a few things that will serve you well. Later in "General Notes on Cooking" you will find another list of things with which any good working kitchen should be outfitted.

Glutened Items Now Off Limits
For Use In Gluten-Free Cooking

wooden cutting board(s) used for
  cutting regular bread
spaghetti pot and colander
metal brownie pan
frying pan that has had breaded or
  dredged foods or pancakes
wooden utensils used for gluten
  cooking

- Heavy frying pan: I do not have a preference as to the brand but just that it is heavy. You may decide to go with a ceramic nonstick surface, but I don't mind stainless steel or the black hard-anodized aluminum, which you can scour.
- 9" × 13" baking pan
- Utensils: (I love the cheap set of bamboo tools that come with different shapes for stirring and scraping.) You will want to get a new spatula suitable for the surface of your frying pan.
- Heavy stock pot with oven-safe handles. (I know this will be expensive but you will thank yourself, especially if you take the time to find a large and heavy one. You can live without it for a little while but it is going to help you a great deal in the larger and more long term food preparation which I fully explain below.) Some will do fine with a big *slow cooker* instead but I guess I am too old fashioned and feel the heavy pot is more versatile. The slow cooker will be much cheaper to buy so the choice is yours.

Another (and much more expensive) option for these purposes might be one of these new technology *pressure cookers* on the market, which have different settings capable of different types of cooking. I think that they are slow cookers as well as able to cook certain foods much quicker than conventional ways but I have never used one. I still prefer my big heavy stockpot because I know what it can do and I like its simplicity.

Late in the writing of this book, I had decided to finally break down and get an air fryer. This is something that our son had mentioned wanting for the household, as he was cooking more. I decided to actually give it to him for his fourteenth birthday (and I imagine him taking it to college in a few years). He was so excited that he made French fries and some beautiful fried chicken tenders first thing. Of course, we are all enjoying using it because we have found it to be very easy and incredibly satisfying. I fully recommend the biggest one that does all kinds of food, but the smaller ones are good too. It was really worth the expense, but I think that it is not needed in the beginning because fried foods are often breaded with things that are not allowed on the anti-inflammatory diet.

Generally, you need to know that any pan with even hairline scratches WILL hold gluten. Even this molecular level of contamination will ruin all your hard work and good intentions. Wooden spoons are notorious, and that goes for the bamboo chopsticks you may have used in Asian cooking, as regular soy sauce has wheat in it. You may be able to use the ladle that you have, unless, of course, it is scratched. I have kept some of my baking pans because I always use muffin papers with the tin, I use parchment paper to line my half-sheet pans, but I did buy new cooling racks. However, you will not be baking much in the beginning, anyway.

So take heart in the knowledge that as you buy that new frying pan you are in keeping with the beautiful gift you give yourself of renewing your mind and renewing your body to freely go forward on this journey. The only reason you should ever look back might be to remember how unhealthy you had been in your old thinking. You cannot become healthy with old thinking. When you put your new mind-set into action, your commitment to new living shows up in a kitchen free of your intolerances and full of the inspiration for all your new choices.

Refrigerator, Pantry, and Freezer—Oh My!

Everyone benefits from a good fridge cleanout. (I should do this more often—the jams and old salsa jars tend to pile up!) I know that sometimes I save things a little too long or I don't get around to using that chicken broth on which I fully had designs of beautiful soup or liquid for cooking. This is why it is very important to *label*. I will get to that subject soon.

Step 1: Clear out. In order to clear out all the things that contain gluten, you have to know what you are looking for. You must learn to read ingredient labels and, in some cases, to call the manufacturers to ask the right questions.

Step 2: Scrub. To avoid any cross contamination from prior messes it is important to really wash all the insides of your cabinets and shelving in storage areas. You can be contaminated by just a small amount of flour which ends up on the outside of the container of acceptable food and then transfers to your hands or drops into something you are preparing. Likewise, if there are things that you will continue using, make sure to wipe down the entire outside of the packaging before replacing them in your new clean space.

Step 3: Only buy gluten-free. You will not be tempted to eat the wrong things if you don't buy them! This is more difficult in a mixed house where you would seriously separate the gluten containing things from everything else, but I hope to encourage you so much in the renewing of your mind that even the presence of gluten will not tempt you. Now that you will cook for yourselves, it becomes clear that by cooking with whole foods (instead of processed ready-mades) it is very easy to avoid gluten.

## What to Throw Away

Obviously, any food passé should be removed but let us look into the average fridge. Regular soy sauce is no good because it is made with wheat. You may have salad dressings, barbecue sauces, mustard, ketchup, and even marinara and salsas, which are contaminated with ingredients containing gluten. What about pudding, potato salad, and a myriad of "kids' food?" But how, dear reader, are you to know what to look for? There are many things that hide gluten innocently passing as some sort of flavoring or food enhancement.

## How to Read Labels

As you discover the landscape of your new life you will learn how to read labels. Gluten has some secret code words which "food" manufacturers use in their ingredient labels. Never eat anything with modified food starch (unless this is followed immediately by something other than wheat) or MSG (you wouldn't eat this anyway because it is an excitotoxin—as also is aspartame—which inflames the brain as well as every other tissue of the body,[20] but it could also be made from wheat). The next buzzwords to look for are binders, confectioner's glaze, caramel color, or natural flavors. It is wise to call the manufacturer to ask if these are made from any gluten-containing ingredients.

This brings me to the faithful practice of looking for those fateful words, which may lie at the bottom of the label often following "allergen information": "made in a facility—or on equipment—that also processes wheat." It is prudent that you steer

### Questions for Manufacturers

Do you use any gluten-containing ingredients in your product(s)?

Are your binders, confectioner's glaze, caramel color, or natural flavors made from any gluten-containing sources?

For topical products: Is your (ingredient: such as tocopherol, tocopheryl acetate, or vitamin E) obtained from any gluten-containing plants/sources?

If they say that they do not know, do not trust.

---

[20] "Foods that Harm, Foods that Heal" Author & Editor, Blaylock, Russell L., MD, The Blaylock Wellness Report, Vol. 14 No. 1, Jan. 2017, Newsmax Media, Inc.

clear of such products. This may be the most disappointing thing of all when one can see by the ingredients that the product could very well be safe to eat. There are whole companies, which I wish would take to heart the importance of zero gluten and create true separation in their processes. This is beginning to happen but slowly. Some companies do work very hard to separate equipment but must indicate it is in the same facility. I have called many companies and urge you to do the same. The more calls they get with the questions we ask, the more they have to consider changing the way things are done.

The pantry door looms—or as the case may be, the next thing is to go through every cabinet and dry goods storage area in your house. Not only must you categorically give or throw away all the pasta, noodles, crackers, and snack foods containing gluten, but you must also make these areas clean.

Here is a list of the actual foods that contain gluten:

* pasta
* whole-wheat pasta
* all-purpose flour
* cake flour
* whole-wheat flour
* durum
* semolina
* farina
* spelt
* bulgar
* triticale
* kamut
* einkorn
* freekah
* farro
* rye
* barley
* malt or malt flavoring
* couscous
* oats or oat flour that does not specify "gluten-free." Although oats do not actually contain gluten they are usually contaminated at some point in the process, such as in milling, packaging on assembly line, and even in their transportation. This is because the processing of oats often happens in the same place and on the same equipment as the processing of wheat.

Oh yes, my friend, the pile of this stuff on the table in my basement absolutely towered! I was especially dismayed because I had been stocking up. I knew that prices were going to go up, and I also feel this protective strain in me, which tends to want to prepare. (Okay, I am not quite a doomsday prepper, but I do think about such things from time to time.) I am happy to say that I had a friend who was in great need and this boatload of food was very welcome. I also gave her my freezer items.

Have you looked into your freezer? This is a wonderful place to store up all kinds of glutenous things! I had two big shopping bags full of pasta, spanakopita, appetizers, and desserts. It is a shame, knowing how many good frozen ready-made dinners have wheat ingredients. But be brave, intrepid wayfarers! Soon that freezer will hold only the cleanest of meat, poultry, fish, and vegetables and all the wonderful creations you will discover how to make yourselves!

## III) Standing Firm

> It is for freedom that Christ has set us free. Stand firm, then, and do
> not let yourselves be burdened again by a yoke of slavery.
>
> —Galatians 5:1

This may be a small section, but you will find it to be of equal if not of the utmost importance among the subjects of this guide. I have written this book in bits and parts with the hope that you will not just read it once but really use it, mark it and write in it, use it to find new resources for not only your sustenance but also your mind-set. I believe that it may be particularly prudent for you read this section every time you go out to any gathering of family or friends.

So many times I hear, "when we go to someone else's place to eat, we do not want to offend or hurt that person's feelings" as a reason someone fell off the gluten-free wagon. This is often true, but sometimes it may just be the last vestige of an excuse to break down. Do not let it be so! We are here, again, on the cutting edge. We may feel like lonely travelers in a wasteland bereft of any good thing to eat but we persevere. Our whole life and health depend on this perseverance. Usually we know exactly what to expect in these cases so it is prudent, first of all, to eat before we leave the house.

Secondly, if possible, it is smart to bring something that could be shared with the whole group. There must be clear in your mind the knowledge of and commitment to your way of life. If someone were serving shrimp cocktail, would he or she expect the one with a shellfish allergy to eat it? Or what about peanuts to the peanut allergic? No. Okay, we do not go into anaphylactic shock needing immediate medical attention, but it *is* that serious. So many are silently suffering—and dying—because of silent or unmentionable symptoms. Do not let this be your fate. One contamination could very well be the one that causes your genetic makeup to turn the corner to autoimmune mayhem. If you already suffer from one (as is true with my husband Steve, who has psoriasis) it could be another nail in your coffin!

In the case that some well-meaning aunt has gone to the trouble to cook you something "gluten-free" in a well-loved but contaminated pan, using butter and you also avoid dairy, *don't* eat it. This is very difficult, but it may be your only teaching moment. And a moment of hurt is really okay if you can be gentle but firm, explaining (hopefully in short) that you cannot eat it. If you think that someone might do this for you, *before* the day you should ask them not to, or at least, go through the whole list of questions on how they should prepare it.

Although I really try to avoid using aluminum as much as possible at home, a cheap foil pan is an easy way for the person to start with a clean pan. They will probably balk at the staying power of gluten in metal pans and wooden spoons. That is another offense—that you would think that they do not clean their pots and utensils. At this point, it may help to just say that you will bring something. There is really no way around it and we may still offend or have to eat clandestinely in the car, but you have to break it to them somehow, sometime. The sooner the better. You do not want to be several months into your awesome new life never having thought about this conversation.

While you are tested daily as each meal comes along, you will be tested the most during occasions of great gathering and emotion. Momentous events: birthdays, weddings, anniversaries, funerals, bar and bat mitzvahs, baptisms, Thanksgiving, Hanukkah, Christmas, and Valentine's Day, just to name a few, all come with their own level of stress depending on as many circumstances as there are humans. Be strong. Stand firm. You are not alone.

# Section 3

# CHAPTER 5

# The Approach to Food

Ants are creatures of little strength, yet they store up their food in the summer.
—Proverbs 30:25

By wisdom a house is built, and through understanding it is established;
through knowledge its rooms are filled with rare and beautiful treasures.
—Proverbs 24:3–4

## I) Looking Ahead

A lot of your success is going to depend on planning ahead. My mother always described her bread baking demonstration at the church festival she's been doing for more than two decades as a pipeline. In bread baking there are just a few steps but each one takes some time. You have to wait for the yeast to proof. You mix up the dough and then you have to wait for it to rise. And after you create the loaves you have to let it rise again. Then of course there is baking time. (I know! Why in the world would I use a *bread* analogy? Because when we grew up, Mom baked bread twice a week and it was magnificent! Oh, how I wish I could still eat it!)

This analogy corresponds to making your dinners. Instead of hours, your pipeline can take place over days, with an eye towards what you will do with the different things you make for the week or the freezer. For example, you might have butternut squash with your dinner one night and maybe you baked it in the morning or the night before. (Baking fresh squash or pumpkin is much easier than you might think. See my how-to!) It is easily warmed up quickly for dinner but it is also really great for soup later. (Look for my "Butternut Squash and Bean Soup.")

Baked potatoes are wonderful to use again. You bake enough extra so that you can make them into home fried potatoes in the morning. The same can be done when you boil lots of potatoes for mashers one night. If you are really industrious and have the ingredients and time together the next day you can make shepherd's pie. (My recipe for "Shepherd's Pie" is included.) While you are at it make a little one in a small oven dish for the freezer.

When you are making extra for the freezer always label it. I often put the food into the oven dish, which will eventually be put into the oven and so it may not have a suitable sealable lid. I always try to put parchment between the food and the plastic wrap with which it is sealed. Not only does this keep food from the BPAs but it also serves to take up any air-space. I usually use two or three layers of plastic and apply the label to the first layer so that it cannot come off in the freezer.

## II) Leftovers? Sounds Like a Bad Word!

For you know the grace of our Lord Jesus Christ, that though he was rich,
yet for your sakes he became poor, so that you through his poverty might become rich.
—2 Corinthians 8:9

I know that some people cannot stand the sight of leftovers and never consider saving anything. I, on the contrary, think of leftovers as resources. The half-cup of mushrooms and onions from the night before becomes instant omelet innards the next morning. The same goes for that extra bit of steamed spinach that nobody took. I love to use steak for my chili— so I buy an extra steak with that plan in mind while shopping. It is much easier to remove the fat and cut them if they have already been broiled. (See my "Steak Chili" recipe.) All this really just serves to illustrate my approach to cooking. We are so blessed by modern refrigeration! Some might consider this using leftovers but it is really a technique of cooking ahead.

Another example is this: I know we will not all eat the whole slab of salmon I purchase along with the shrimp for our dinner. Everybody else would rather have shrimp and Steve and I eat some of the salmon. About half of this beautiful fish is left after dinner so I just refrigerate it. It is cooked as per my "Simple Salmon Bake." The next day I make the cold fish into my "Salmon-Egg Salad"—even more convenient if I have the eggs already hard-boiled in the icebox. It is so easy to mix up for lunch or snacks and no fish is wasted—a welcome change from tuna salad and there is not the same danger of heavy metals. Cooking real food does require some extra planning, but when you get going this way, along with proper date labeling and the use of lists to remind you what resides behind the fridge door, you will be easily making so much good food you won't know what to do with it!

What I am trying to put across is that, whether you cook for yourself or for your whole family, you should try always to cook for the future. Not only does this save time, but it also will save you trips to the store and it will save you money.

Long before I discovered that I, and the rest of the family, would have to change our diets I wanted to write a cookbook called *Back to the Basics*. I am often surprised by the lack of interest in some people to cook for themselves or their families. I know that time may constrain some people in certain ways, but it may be that the family has not taken the problem to heart and found the viable options. When it is urgent and necessary that the diet be changed, as in the case of gluten intolerance, these options *must* be explored and the problem of cooking be solved.

I have always loved (and still do love and use) the *Joy of Cooking* because it holds so much wisdom and practical knowledge from the history of cooking and ingredients. I guess I really want to know why and how. I can appreciate the new editions which include some modern dishes and a refreshed look, but I love my, my mother's, and my grandmother's editions for the original, if maybe unhealthy or forgotten, recipes that may have gone out of style, because of the elementary processes they describe. I went back to *The Joy* when I wanted to learn how to make marmalade because I did not trust the quick instructions inside the box of pectin. From that book I was able to make it my own and feel confident about its authenticity.

Okay, that was really a subject for another book, but I want to let you know, dear reader, that there are many ways to do things. I choose to make things from scratch because I know what they are made of and they taste better. When you make your own barbecue sauce, it not only tastes better, but it *is* better. The same goes for very simple things such as chicken broth or mashed potatoes. When you go to the ready-mades you will always find too much salt, sugar, and unhealthy additives, which serve only to thicken, preserve, or even just make it look better. That is not food. The "time-saving" processed foods make and keep us unhealthy and eventually put us in the hospital.

The SAD diet has not only made Americans unhealthy, but it has narrowed the view of what to eat. When our family got through the difficult beginnings and began to build up and expand our repertoire of things to eat, we had already changed our view of what is something appropriate to snack on or to have as a meal. You can do this too! We were afraid to eat outside our home for some time after we had reintroduced all the foods we can tolerate. But as we learned the questions to ask and even what a "safe" place to eat "looks" like we regained our freedom and then some!

Not being addicted to gluten anymore empowered us to look beyond fast food "staples" (which are not staples at all). Not that we really ever relied on so much fast food, but I am talking about this silly idea that we need bread at every meal, a roll or two pieces of bread to hold a sandwich together, pasta and baked goods as whole meals! This is far from the truth but it remains unseen because people are conditioned to accept that one must have a bagel or a muffin for breakfast. As Drs. Davis and Perlmutter, just to name a couple of well-known voices of the many crying in the desert, have amply shown, these foods, in addition to being gluten, turn into too much sugar for our bodies to process.

## III) Organic?

I praise you because I am fearfully and wonderfully made;
your works are wonderful, I know that full well.

—Psalm 139:14

To go "completely organic" is actually quite difficult, both physically and fiscally. However, the choices are greater than you may think. If you keep your diet very simple, as in, including very few foods, you could probably do it but you might get bored of your menu very quickly. Sometimes the choices of actual organic produce in the supermarket are quite lacking, and you might only end up with green onions, grape tomatoes (only after you've finished the healing elimination diet), carrots, and lettuce—which actually sound like a great salad. You could really live on this, but as is evident in any grocery store, we Americans really want variety.

You should know that there is a great list at www.ewg.org called the "Dirty Dozen and Clean 15," a guide issued every year by an organization that tests all kinds of produce every year. It means that you may not have to actually buy everything organic to have variety in your diet.

I often base my meal decisions on what looks good. That goes, not only for fruits and vegetables, but also for the meats. I am sure you have heard of "seasonal cooking." Well, it should be done as much as possible. I was thrilled yesterday to find the organic grapes are back in my store, the bag of which actually has printed on it, "May–July." Also, they were not all that expensive because it is their season. We do without them except for once in a while during the rest of the year.

Another thing is not to disdain the frozen food departments. Blueberries, which are not actually on the dirty dozen list as of the last couple of years, have in the past been notorious for pesticide contamination. However, a wonderful thing is to buy frozen organic blueberries and they are actually cheaper than the fresh commercial ones. I do buy conventionally grown berries if I know the grower. It is always important to wash all your fruits and vegetables, even your organic produce, as there are still organic pesticides used.

There is a great upside to all of this: A doctor I know, who uses nutritional response therapy, reassures me that when our bodies are in good health because we have healed and try to eat organic *most* of the time, our bodies are then able to process and remove the many toxins we encounter in our environment and our foods over which we do not have control.

## IV) How in the World Can I Possibly Make this Work?

Surely God is my help; the Lord is the one who sustains me.

—Psalm 54:4

Time is really the most precious commodity. Yes, fresh whole foods take longer to prepare than the ready-made and processed foods. Yes, you may have to get up in the morning a little bit earlier to cut some vegetables so you can get dinner together more quickly when you come home. I work hard to provide more nutritional food for my family because the long-term healthful benefits far outweigh the slight inconvenience. We cannot give up the proper fueling of the body because it would compromise our ability to finish life with health and vitality, the natural result of eating superior foods, which are far more nutritionally dense.

I have made cooking a pastime and you might consider this. Instead of hating to cook and clean, it can become an art within the family. Undeniably, we are all in it together. There are many ways to make short work of it if you can delegate just a few jobs. Not only this, but it is also important that the young take an interest in what you are doing so that they will be able to fend for themselves when they are not with you. All it really requires is some good planning and creativity. This may take some practice but after a while it gets easier.

I talked to a mother recently who used a spreadsheet to plan her family's meals every Thursday, shopped on Friday, and then got together with her sister to cook on Saturday for the week. That is not how I do it, but it sounds like a wonderful routine to get it done and eat the best food that you have cooked yourself! There are many ways to do this, but, no matter what your planning practice is, it is very important to have an eye to the future keeping in mind what can be accomplished each day.

# CHAPTER 6

# Meal Planning and Shopping: Planning Ahead

Finish your outdoor work and get your fields ready; after that, build your house.
—Proverbs 24:27

Lists are definitely our friends! I make all kinds of lists. But honestly, for me, planning dinners ahead has almost always been a general activity in the grocery store. I go by what looks good, or what may be on sale, and what they have available. I try to think of two or three dinners and some things that I will use for snacking and lunches.

At home, sometimes it helps me to make a list in the morning of the things (dishes) we will have for the dinner that night. This way, I don't forget anything. I especially do this if I am to be entertaining or bringing food out for a picnic or potluck. So other than the reminding lists of the things needed that we use daily, more of my brainstorming, list making and meal planning actually happens during or after I have shopped. I love **self-sticking notes** because it is a benefit to put a list of the things that are *in* the refrigerator *on* the fridge. It can become difficult to remember when there

## How to Avoid GMO Foods

Popcorn is never a GMO and fresh sweet corn in the summer is almost all non-GMO. However, there have been more strains of GMO sweet corn grown lately so you should ask the grower. And you should pop your own popcorn because the butter flavoring in the packages and movie popcorn has a terrible chemical in it. In the grocery store, look for the flower logo with the words "non-GMO certified." Choose organic corn, organic soy, and organic canola. Avoid sugar beets and look for the words "cane sugar" instead. That said, if you want to really know the low-down on GMOs, I refer you to Jacqueline Peppard's book, *New Era Healthy Eating*—she really explains what canola oil is. Also, choose organic green and yellow summer squashes. Check out nongmoshoppingguide.com.

are some leftovers to manage. There is also a bit more of a thought process for me as I might have to go several places to buy the things that we need.

Generally, our grocery store serves us well because it has a good gluten-free selection and some availability of organic meat, produce, and other products. However, there are things that I know I can only find in another store, which is farther away, such as things in the bulk food store, and things I can only get at the health food store. You have to look. Some items I have also found are best bought in an Asian food store. To help you get started, here are some ideas:

The health food store will always have a wider selection of just about everything you may want; however, you are going to pay a premium price. It is good to peruse the aisles just to see what they have to offer and there may be something you cannot do without that you also cannot find anywhere else near you. If you have a more upscale grocery store, you might find some of those items there. Some people find it very good to order certain things such as non-gluten flours online. There are also some marvelous companies from which you can order online and they send their delicious gluten-free baked goods frozen.

My Asian market happens to be an excellent Korean-owned establishment with all manner of exciting Asian goodies. Not only do I find interesting greens, mushrooms, and vegetables for a better price than in my grocery store, but also, there are some exotic things to be found for the flavoring and fortifying of your meals (which you might have considered sadly lacking because of mandatory omissions of major foods).

You will find noodles you can eat which are not all made of corn. Sweet potato starch noodles—if only I had known about these when on the elimination diet! Of course there are all kinds of rice noodles of different sizes and shapes, but I personally love what are called bean threads made from mung beans—tiny fine vermicelli which takes about a minute to cook! You will probably find dried mung beans too. One time I made humus out of them; not bad—really more like a bean dip.

Another excellent place to look, here, is in the canned food shelves where super-hot red and green curry pastes and other hot chili sauces can be found. (I do warn you that these are not for the uninitiated—you must be able to withstand the fire of very spicy peppers!) The main thing, though, when looking in this section, is that you must read the ingredients in search of those gluten derivatives used in so many places.

You will find the familiar Asian vegetables such as water chestnuts, baby corn, straw mushrooms, and others for a better price than the grocery. Tamari sauce and gluten-free soy sauce is cheaper in the Asian store than the grocery store. I prefer tamari sauce for the taste, but in addition, gluten-free soy sauce usually contains rice. Also, do not miss the cans of coconut milk, Chinese cooking wine, and sesame oil.

So, dear reader, there are lots of lists to be made, some investigation and comparison shopping to be done in the beginning, but you will soon learn your own way to make your shopping as swift and convenient as possible.

# CHAPTER 7

# Gluten-Free Living with the Children

Train up a child in the way he should go, and when he is oldhe will not turn from it.
—Proverbs 22:6

## I) Reflections of Ourselves

Before I get into the lifestyle and practice of the subject of this book concerning your young children, I would like to take a little time here to show you, dear reader, my view of feeding/teaching children in general. It is very easy to teach your children to eat, and even like, a variety of healthful foods. You must simply show them how *you* enjoy vegetables and other so-called "adult" foods. There must be repetition and variation over time to help a child to learn to like good things. I know that the common approach is trying things several times over time, but if the parent is eating something else the child will want that instead because he is no dummy! Some things such as spicy or highly aromatic foods may be too adult for him (at first…) but this idea that kids have to have "kids' food" *is the problem.* "Kids' food" is usually very bland with plenty of salt, sugar, and fried grease, none of which is good for *anyone* on a regular basis. (Oh, by the way, these things are what feed and multiply the bad bacteria in our gut.) It breaks my heart that this accepted method of feeding children in restaurants, at home, and at school only serves to attune the children's taste to these incredibly unhealthy choices, setting them up for obesity and disease from the beginning!

Yes, this is going to require some work on the part of the parent—perhaps even an honest look at what Mom and/or Dad is eating. We all need to be wary of what goes into the body because it is not just a matter of energy, but nutrition is the driver of a whole team of processes, which each can be destructive or beneficial in the long run. Even if *you* have the attitude that you'll die anyway, *your child has the right to his or her best chance of life.*

Your life has changed. Now that you and your family are eating gluten-free, it is time to be creative. Children adapt to this lifestyle more easily than we give them credit for doing. It is up to us as parents to make it simple and very matter-of-fact. They will get used to it much faster if there is no longer any gluten in your home.

One way to gain the agreement of your school-aged kids is to take them shopping with you. Let them pick food items that are not only substitutes for their favorites, but also, new unthought-of choices. My children pick out the gluten-free cereals or muffin mixes to make for breakfast or snacking. But they have also found a new love for sausage or avocado at breakfast, which I like because it is always better to start the day with protein and good fats instead of all carbohydrates. Don't forget that eggs or French toast are pretty quick to make, and with good organization one can make bacon to go with them. If enough is made I then put BLTs in their lunches that day. The trick is to make the toast, butter it, and let it cool while I make breakfast. The bacon and lettuce go in the sandwich but I always pack the tomato separately so that it does not soak the bread. They also have definite preferences when it comes to the chips and cookies for other snacks and treats. The main thing is to find the things they can really enjoy and include them wherever it is possible.

Here is some straight talk from a friend of mine who has been seriously making it work in her family:

My youngest is ten years old and he reads labels. I put the responsibility on him. That way he can see for himself if something is allowed in the shopping cart or not and I am not the bad guy telling him "no." At first, it was very hard to not give in. I didn't want my children to feel different or lose out on the foods they loved. Then I realized I wasn't doing them any favors by allowing them to eat a substance that damaged their health.

I started telling myself that I wouldn't allow them to have peanut butter cookies or crackers if they were allergic to peanuts. Of course, with an allergy you see an outward reaction, with gluten intolerance you do not. Perhaps that is what makes it challenging at first to be committed to gluten-free eating. If nothing bad seems to happen as a result of eating gluten then isn't it okay? No, it is not, and here is why: Even kids get leaky gut from the compounded introduction of gluten.

How to get a kid to swallow a pill:

The inevitable taking of pills began because, in the beginning, my daughter *had* to take some other supplements with each meal as well as the probiotic in the morning. There was no way around it. Unfortunately, we lose our nutrition in the process of not knowing that we are gluten intolerant. You and I have no trouble taking a good whole-food multivitamin, or a probiotic capsule, but how do you teach a child to do this? Now, some of the best EFA

DHA supplements are by dropper and supposed to be flavored with citrus or something, but I could only torture the kids with that for so long (actually they stuck it out for almost a year). One has to take two to three big gel capsules a couple times a day to get the same as 1 ml (dropper) of the good stuff.

The kids had a liquid vitamin concoction in the beginning, which my son did not mind but my daughter grimaced or tried to get me to forget it every single morning and night! Later, we could no longer get the liquid for some reason, so we tried the chewables, which they hated even more. (That was a waste of money. I kept thinking I could sneak them into smoothies but deep down I know they'll ruin anything they touch!) So I went back to our doctors and by then these two intrepid kids were veteran pill-takers so they told me we could switch to a half-dose of whole food multivitamins for adults.

The best way to start is to choose some food like potato, sweet potato, applesauce, or squash—maybe even a mouthful of rice. The child is directed to chew a mouthful of said food for a few moments without swallowing it, he or she then takes the pill or capsule into the mouth and the whole thing is swallowed at once. After this is done over and over with each necessary supplement the child decides one day to try it with liquid. It may not be successful right away, but with a little perseverance every child can do this because the food way is annoying and time-consuming.

## II) Gluten-Free in Public—the Questions to Ask

For your kids, it is the same as it is for you. When eating out in restaurants or convenience stores, they will know what to do. If the child is too young to be in control, you will provide his or her snacks and fully inform any caregiver or friend's parent of your child's dietary requirements. Because you have laid strong groundwork in the redirection of your family's diet, given each and every one of them the empowerment of knowledge, your older children who might be without you while visiting with friends or at school functions, will know the questions to ask.

Much like those questions that we ask the manufacturers of food mentioned in section 2, we ask questions concerning food preparation in restaurants mainly to have them hear them. The questions must go beyond, "Are there any gluten-containing ingredients in this dish?" There is still much unknown to servers, managers, line cooks and even chefs who have been in the business a long time. As you have learned in the Battle Plan Section, there is much ado about *cooking surfaces and utensils*.

For instance, you might ask, "Do you ever put bread on the grill?" or "Can you cook that in a pan that has never had gluten such as pancakes or dredged meat?" Often, you will be met with indignation, as your words seem to question their ability (or lawfulness) in sanitation, a major requirement for any food service.

When you go to restaurant chains or cafeteria-style places (if you dare) you tell them that you are gluten intolerant "so I need you to please change your gloves." If there is a corn tortilla involved and you just have to have it warmed, tell them put foil between the sides of the tortilla and the cooking surfaces. Personally, I go for the "bowl" option. There is the thought that they will touch the handles of utensils, which have been touched by gloves that touched wheat tortillas. However, one time I was at one of these in the mall and I was very happy to see them grab a new serving spoon for every item I wanted in my bowl. Thank them for their good practices when you get to the cash register. As you can see, there are many places for pitfalls if you go out to eat. Even if every precaution is observed there is still a high probability that you could be contaminated.

One surefire and deciding question is to ask if their French fries are cooked in oil separate from that used for any type of breaded fried food (such as onion rings, chicken fingers, fried shrimp, etc.). If so, do not order them. You may ask if their fries are gluten-free—because some frozen fries are actually breaded—but you *must* also ask the question about the oil in which they are fried. This is more of an exercise for the purpose of awareness so don't get upset if they don't have separate fryers. Many restaurants are just unable to cover the expense to put in more than one. One well-known fast food chain does have a policy of separate fryers, but the strictness with which that policy is followed varies from store to store. For example, the onion rings are right in the next bin under the heat lamps and can easily fall into the French fries.

Another thing to watch for in a Mexican restaurant is, if you have ordered a nice appetizer of guacamole, chips and salsa, and the corn chips come to the table hot. If you did not ask before, you *must* ask if these chips were fried in the same oil in which wheat tortillas have been fried. Do not eat them if they were. So sad, I know. But you can probably get some cold un-fried chips to go with your food. In addition, it is important that you specify that you want a corn tortilla because some people do not actually know that a regular flour tortilla is wheat.

Sushi can be a great thing to enjoy out as long as they do not add flour to the rice (which I think only happens in very cheap places). Ask about it. When you go, bring your own bottle of tamari (and maybe some salad dressing—or ask for oil and vinegar because of the possibility there). I have only found one pan-Asian place (blessedly nearby) that serves miso made without soy sauce. So that is a question you should always ask, is the soup made with soy sauce? Thai curries by their nature do not have soy sauce, but one should be aware that the pan it's cooked in is most likely contaminated with it. Our little neighborhood place is owned by a knowledgeable person who may have food issues herself so we feel quite safe, as there is good understanding of the pitfalls.

You can see where I have been going with this…a Chinese restaurant is really not a safe place because a great deal of the cooking involves soy sauce. I have read suggestions of the few things one might be able to eat, but as all the cooking surfaces are thoroughly inundated with gluten, I would not recommend it. We do not go to Chinese. If you only wanted tea it would be perfectly safe.

My children often wisely choose not to eat anything where there are snacks provided because they know that is the safest and they can eat when they get home. I try very hard not to let this happen and so I either send them out with full bellies and/or send them with food. But again, these great kids know how to read the labels! If they are offered whole fruit or single serving enclosed snacks of safe foods, they know they can eat them. Thankfully, there are certain households in which there is no fear of contamination because the parents are fully aware and know how to provide for our kids. This is because we have laid the groundwork there as well. If you can help them understand about food prep surface contamination some care so much that they go out of their way to do it right. That is such a relief!

Parties and celebrations are the same—let them eat before they go and take gluten-free items to share. Ours have gotten so used to everything that they focus on the festivities not the food.

One more thing here is that, unfortunately if you insist on going out, there is a terribly high probability that you will be contaminated. Our doctors have always told us that if we go out (granted that we would only choose truly gluten-free foods—no cheating!) we should always take our GlutenFlam. I have found since, that this may be controversial, as I have run into comments by people who do not believe gluten-and-dairy-destroying enzymes work. I do not know which one(s) they used, but we have always had a good response using the one that our doctors gave us. In fact, it was incorporated into the healing supplement regimen with every single meal while we were on the elimination diet. We take it if we eat anything prepared outside our home and if we haven't and we come home with that terrible feeling, we take it as soon as possible and maybe again at the next few meals. We keep some capsules in each of the cars so it is always nearby.

*Lunch idea for elementary to middle school that needs a cookie or another little treat*

*Full sandwiches for high schoolers would each be accompanied by one or two snacks*

## III) What to Do about Lunches!

School lunch may be one of the most difficult hurdles you face because you must think of everything. So instead of bemoaning the fact that they will not eat hot lunches provided by the school and therefore lunch is not your problem, you need to change your mind-set about it. Remember, you are on the cutting edge—and so your children are too! Your example of positive reinforcement in the whole thinking about this change in your lives will be visible to and teaching your kids. This is your excellent new life—for *all* of you!

Along with breakfast you will need to allow time for the making of lunch—unless you manage to do it the night before as my husband always wanted me to do. (I occasionally do that and still hope to improve.) I want to interject how sad I am to hear from my kids how many of their friends go without breakfast! Mine never do that and it would be disastrous if they did because it is so important to fuel for an even metabolism. So there *must* be time. There is no excuse—and if they have to, they should eat it on the way to school.

As I said earlier, protein and good fats (think brain food) at breakfast are key. They last longer than carbohydrates alone. There should be some in their lunches also. There is nothing wrong with peanut butter and jelly once in a while. Ethan does not love peanut butter like Nina does so I might give him a chicken or turkey sandwich. That said, I actually do not often give them sandwiches in their lunches (the bread *is* very expensive and they were never really sandwich kids anyway). And now that Ethan cannot really have rice on a regular basis I pack him chicken, pork or steak from our dinner cut, and ready to eat. So here is a little list of our lunch ideas, which I try to vary and mix so that most of the food groups (the good ones) are covered:

- apple slices with peanut butter
- lentil chips and hummus
- corn chips and salsa (and/or hummus)
- cut-up chicken, pork, or steak from the night before with salt and pepper or whatever they like to dip it in on the side
- cut-up hot dog* or hamburger with ketchup and/or mustard on the side
- bacon and tomato (packed separately so the bacon doesn't get soggy) "wraps" using some nice romaine leaves for the wrap
- rolled deli meats (not too often if they contain nitrates)
- cheese and GF crackers
- homemade soup, chili or pasta in a thermos, cheese on the side
- cold cooked green beans with "Tamari-Ginger Sauce" on the side to dip in
- chopped cucumber or carrots and celery

- tomato salad (two different recipes later in this book)
- Pasta Salad with Black Beans
- easy fruit like a plum, banana, a couple of clementines or strawberries, or cut fruit like pineapple, melon, or sliced orange
- SALAD with their favorite dressing ready to pour on

### BPA-Free

Some people are adamant about ridding their households and lives of this dangerous toxin, which leaches out of everyday plastics. One of the worst things you can do is to freeze a bottle of water for your summer day—seems so convenient, I know. I think that it is very difficult to completely remove all bad plastics and will be impractical. My answer is to use glass or ceramic for storage of leftovers wherever possible. I still use plastic bags but try to limit them.

Nina loves feta and a few olives on hers. Ethan will have some deli sliced turkey or ham and cheese with crackers packed separately from the salad.

The main thing is that everything should be *ready to eat* so no time is wasted at lunchtime (like, for instance, having to peel the orange). This seems like a lot of work, but if you know what they like and pack it the way they like it they will eat it. This is why it is important to find the little BPA free plastic lunch box pieces. And don't forget to put in any utensils that they will need. In my experience of late, I have found that there is often much less time for them to eat their lunches than might be supposed. Anything you can do to have everything they eat ready to eat when they open their lunchboxes will go a long way toward the goal of them actually eating it! My daughter has been packing her own lunch a lot more lately, which I love. But I don't mind doing it as long as I have what I need because of good planning.

### PIZZA!

Sometimes I prepare GF pizzas the night before. There are some rice free GF tortilla wraps, which work well for pizzas as well as the ready-made pizza crusts which all seem to contain dairy and/or rice. This is especially good to do if I know that there is going to be a pizza day at school for everyone else. This is very important. Once, I did not have the time or what I needed, so I talked the gourmet pizza guy into making my kids' special GF pizzas earlier than they opened (he was so sweet about it). Some of the other kids were actually envious of what I left for my kids at school that day! Sure, it was a splurge, but sometimes making an effort like that can mean the world to these kids who never asked to have their diets changed and can't have a common pretzel with everyone else! Can't even be touched by their friends until they have washed that common pretzel off! I am thankful and confident that my kids are so aware that they even watch for what people have on their hands and know how to protect their own food or not to eat it if it has become contaminated. Kids are amazing! They can do it!

*Hot dogs: Although they are not the healthiest option, if not eaten very regularly, we do enjoy a certain brand that is gluten-free, but chances are that there is some GMO material within. I have tried to get them to eat the various small brands of "natural" hot dogs to no avail. (If you can get yours to eat these instead, bravo!)

## IV) Snacks and Treats

It is very important to pack things they can grab at other times than lunch because they should never be hungry. Yes, that means some junk food like potato chips and sweet things. They're kids! I did bring mine up to eat the good stuff first—they actually want to eat the substantial things because they know how bad they feel if they don't. If your kids are more apt to eat the junk first, just put one cookie or one sweet thing in (without the potato chips) and extra "sides" so that they eat the healthy stuff because they are still hungry. Anyone can learn to like healthy foods. It just takes time.

### Corn Snacks

When faced with the choice between commercial corn chips and commercial popcorn, always choose the popcorn. They have not modified it genetically because it is not worth their while! However, the popcorn may be cooked in soybean or canola oil and is therefore not non-GMO and the butter flavoring (especially on microwave and movie popcorn) is extremely bad for humans.

## V) School Birthday Celebrations

This subject is really most important with kids of elementary school age when the moms are sending in a dozen beautiful cupcakes piled high with ready-made frosting. So that your child does not lack in special treats a great thing to do is to make a normal-sized batch of chocolate cupcakes—or whatever your child's favorite kind is—and you freeze them. You are not going to have to make a whole batch every time and you will always be ready for when there is a celebration of any kid's birthday in school.

There is always a freezer somewhere (might be the faculty lounge) that can house your kid's special cupcakes. Only send in about four at a time, make sure to label them with your child's name, and keep tabs with your kid on how many are left. Hopefully you know or will find out when there are celebrations. Those days you can send your child in with an individual amount of delicious homemade frosting in a plastic bag. Or you can just put the individual bags of icing into the same bag with the frozen cupcakes. It takes very little time to soften this small amount of icing for use. It is so easy and fun for him to just clip the very tip off the corner of the bag and apply the icing himself. The rest of it will probably go directly into his mouth—what fun! Of course, when it's your own child's birthday, he has an opportunity to share with the whole class and show how delicious gluten-free can be!

Our daughter Nina has largely taken charge of her own eating for years. She often reads the labels better than I now and has saved me from my own imprudence on several occasions. It was very hard for her in the beginning at the age of ten and for several more of these formative years some things remained difficult among her peers. I am so very proud of her faithfulness to this program for her health. I feel quite assured that she will remain gluten-free because of her great knowledge and independence. Nina, by the age of fourteen was already an excellent cook and I love to eat what she makes. She also has given me, here, her own statement of her observations from that time:

> Gluten-free people have better appreciation for food than the average person. Anyone who eats gluten can just grab a doughnut for breakfast on the way to work or order some Chinese food when they don't want to cook. But when a restaurant or chain carries gluten-free pizza or just has gluten-free hamburger rolls, gluten-free people are thankful for every bite.

Nina is absolutely right about our appreciation of simple foods, but she and I also agree that gluten-free people can enjoy a wider range of foods *because* they do not resort to the "staples." As you, dear reader, really begin to search out what you and your family like and can eat, you too, will begin to feel the freedom that the knowledge about your food and how it makes you feel inside actually opens up to you!

# CHAPTER 8

# Traveling Wisely and More Eating Out

"See I will send my messenger, who will prepare the way before me."
—Malachi 3:1a

Something very important to think about well ahead of time in order to prepare is what you will do when you go on a trip. Will you travel by car or bus, or have to be even more regimented about the snacks you can carry because you are getting on a plane? Once I was completely upset when an entire unopened tub of hummus was taken away from me by airport security. The same would happen with a container of yogurt. If you will be on a long or overseas flight on which a meal will be served it is very important that you call the airline twenty-four hours in advance to tell them that you want a gluten-free meal. However, there may not be the option to have it also dairy-free so you must be vigilant when the meal comes to you and be careful not to eat anything made with butter or cheese. I *never* expect that they can do what we need and so I *always* carry our own snacks.

What will you do when you get there? Have you an idea of how you can shop for your food or a place to keep it and also to cook it or warm it up? These are very important questions. How about these same questions concerning a camping trip? Or what will your hotel/motel room actually have for your use? If the place you are going does not have the kind of store that would carry GF items, can you send a package to yourself ahead of time?

If you opt for eating out you will be at the mercy of whatever there may be at your destination and in some places that may mean you can only have salad. No matter what the establishment may consider gluten-free (and dairy-free) there is an extremely high probability of cross-contamination and *that is not gluten-free*. By now you have got an idea of what questions to ask but if not, go back to the section with Preparing your Kitchen and also the Gluten-Free with the Children chapter.

I am trying to give you some ideas, but ultimately, this is an exercise in logistics that you cannot ignore if you are thinking of traveling. These are, again, the super-testing times during which you cannot let your guard down no matter where you are. In the beginning you may want to reread parts of this book if you feel you might break down and eat the wrong things. Even where there are special or famous foods it is not worth it. Take care of yourself and set a good example for your loved ones because it matters. Take heart that as time goes by you will know what to ask and what is safe more easily and the good habits and attitudes will be second-nature before too long. Enjoy your surroundings and the people you are with knowing that you are healthy and strong. Enjoy your life!

I am neither a doctor nor a nutritionist, but simply a wife and mother, and I want to be your cheerleader. I have always cooked and I thank God for my parents who never caved to the mainstream lifestyle of fast and convenient, foods. The nutrition contained within the real food supply has always been of great interest to me since I began my own search for true health more than twenty years ago. For over ten years I have been reading about research, which does not appear to be mainstream. However, this information is common knowledge to our own doctors in whose care we have been since our family discovered the gluten intolerance in every one of us. We have learned that there are so many health issues that can be triggered by gluten in the gluten intolerant that it should not be ignored. We should *not* accept as normal a whole list of things, the least of which includes headaches, stomach aches, joint pain, fatigue, skin problems, dental problems, bloating and gas after eating, not to mention the whole AD spectrum and neurological conditions such as brain fog, migraines, anxiety, or sudden emotional outbursts. These things and so many more, including autoimmune diseases, just a few of which are diabetes, fibromyalgia, Parkinson's, and Meniere's disease, can be attributed to gluten as an external factor in their onset. In these cases, therefore, they can be alleviated or avoided entirely with healing and the continued adherence to the diet encouraged in this book.

So here is to you, my friend, open minded enough to read this book in hopes of finding the solution for optimum health, honest enough to be looking this whole gluten phenomenon square in the face, and courageous enough to set to work and follow through with the practical help I have tried to manifest in my life and to demonstrate in this book. May God go with you and bless you every day!

## General Notes on Cooking

As a jam maker, over the years, I have been developing products with an eye towards retaining the nutrition contained in the fruits and vegetables of which my jams, jellies, and sauces are made. I also found a way to use xylitol (which also happens to be a prebiotic) for very satisfying sugar-free versions. In the process of building this business I was educated in sanitation and cross-contamination which, in turn, made me consider these things while cooking for my family.

Safety should be observed in the kitchen at all times. It is important to have some good potholders for removing pans from the oven. Dishtowels are not always enough and if yours is wet you will get burned. Some pot lid handles do heat up in which case you should use a potholder. If a stockpot or frying pan with oven safe handles is being used in the oven it is very easy to forget and just grab one. Don't forget to protect yourself!

One of the rules in a commercial kitchen is to wear closed toed shoes. It is a good idea in case a knife falls. Speaking of knives, it is actually safer to keep them sharp so that little effort is needed. A dull knife can cause trouble because the more effort to cut can lead to inconsistent timing and unpleasant surprises.

*Always* use a cutting board. When I was quite young my mother once said that you can easily slice through and cut your hand when you cut a pepper. Her words have stayed with me and I still think of them every single time I pick up a pepper! It is always safest to cut something on a cutting board (even if you happen to have seen me do it holding the fruit in my hand!)

As I cannot describe good knife skills here very well, I suggest that anyone who is a beginner be slow and methodical. Keep all your fingers strongly *together* on the vegetable. This may be difficult at first but should become second nature. Look for demonstrations of this knife skill on the internet.

Depending on how much cooking you have ventured into in your life, there are a few things that you may already have or want to have for cooking your basic dishes and foodstuffs.

**2-quart saucepan**
**small double boiler** (very useful for melting chocolate or warming foods if you do not have a microwave oven)
**oven-safe dishes or casseroles with covers** in two or three sizes
**square pan** (9"×9" or 8"×8")
**mixing bowls** (at least three or four sizes)—Pyrex type is great because the can be used in the microwave and also be used (carefully) over (not in) a pan of water as a double boiler
one or two **smaller cheap frying pans**
one or two **half-sheet pans**
one or two **cutting boards** (clean!—meaning not having been used for bread)

There should be a **broiler pan** (2 pcs.) that goes with your oven. If not broiling can be done in a half-sheet pan with racks to lift the food up off the bottom.

**strainer**: buy a new one if you have one that has been used to drain pasta

**funnel**

**slotted spoon**

**whisk**

**tongs**

**garlic press**

**peeler**

**a scrub brush dedicated to fruits and vegetables only**

**grater** (A **microplane** is better for lemon zest but the larger holes on a standard grater are necessary for grating potatoes or carrots.)

**measuring cups and spoons**

**toothpicks or wooden skewers**

**parchment paper**

**meat thermometer**

Consider a **mortar and pestle.**

Always read through the entire recipe before beginning—or shopping!

Abbreviations:

T. means tablespoon

t. means teaspoon

EVOO is extra virgin olive oil

Sugar

I never use conventional white sugar. There may be a slight difference in taste and color but I would rather have the phytonutrients present in organic or raw sugar. The cook could also use honey or maple syrup for certain things but they might change the baking time/ consistency of baked goods—and I would never use either for making jam. That said, during the elimination (anti-inflammatory) diet all types of sugar are forbidden to keep the metabolism from spiking and causing stress hormones to be made. After that, we have the choice to reintroduce sugars (because we have missed our desserts) or maybe not. One might actually not be craving them and we do know that sugar is the worst offender causing inflammation. What if we could continue to avoid sugars? It would go a long way to keeping this wonderful health achieved during the intensely restrictive time of elimination.

Salt

When I write or think of salt it is sea salt. I like that there are still trace minerals in unrefined sea salt. I have at times found it necessary to strain the larger particles out or crush it with a mortar and pestle so that it can be incorporated more easily with certain ingredients.

Spices

I order most of my spices from a reputable company because their products do not contain gluten unless it is intrinsic to the product in which case I do not need it. As with everything else one is unsure of it is important to call the company to find out.

Cooking Oils

The first thing I want to establish is that "vegetable oil" is really anything but. It usually refers to corn or canola oils which (unless clearly designated organic or non-GMO) are made from the genetically modified organisms (plants) that have been ingeniously patented so that the corporations owning them have the ability to demand money and retributions from growers who (most likely inadvertently) may have the seeds (or pollen) deposited in their fields simply by the birds and wind. Sounds ridiculous, I know, but it has happened. Sorry, got off on a rant…

These oils (corn and canola) are bad for their own reasons, but also, peanut, sunflower and safflower oils are not that great to cook with on a regular basis because of the high presence of omega-6. It is true that we need a little of this essential fatty acid but it must be in balance with omega-3. So of course, one's mind goes immediately to peanuts, peanut butter and sunflower seeds. I do still eat and give my kids peanut butter (and jam, of course) and we have found some beautiful dairy-free chocolate "peanut butter-like cups" made instead with sunflower seed butter. But these things are in moderation. I just feel it is right to tell you why these oils are not that healthy for cooking.

I have been reading a very informed book, which discusses oils and smoke points with far more depth. I realize now that the avocado oil I get for a good price is definitely not the first cold pressed extra virgin oil that the author sites as the most healthful type of avocado oil because obviously heat has been applied in its refining process. I admire Jacqueline Peppard, whose book, *New Era Healthy Eating*, c. 2017, lays out some very thorough research on ingredients and the toxins that reside within them or not. She uses extra virgin cold pressed olive oil for many of her recipes, as do I. The main thing with this olive oil is not to cook anything at too high a temperature. If it smokes it becomes very bad for you, but under careful watch as things cook it can be a way to ingest a good fat. As I can understand her going fully the distance (with the information that is known so far) to create and eat food without toxins, I hope that any of my readers might rise to her challenge. My aim is to bridge the gap between the average person's desire to be healthy and actual proactive change. Some would be stopped from the complete detoxification put forth by Ms. Peppard simply by the cost of certain things or their unobtainability. Some may want to go the full distance toward clean food to the extent that Peppard does. To both groups I would heartily suggest Peppard's book not only to be informed of the extensive research she has done, but also, for her refined recipes (except, of course, for the few that employ einkorn wheat flour) which do go beyond the more basic foods I have written about in this book.

To return to oils, I agree with Peppard that one should pick an oil which best complements or fits in with the particular recipe as per its ethnic origin. So when stir frying a Chinese-style dish one might still want to use peanut oil and a Thai style dish would benefit from the use of coconut oil. I use avocado oil often because it does not have a strong flavor.

Off the subject again, but it seems to follow here, is that this is the very reason that commercial beef is so bad for us. It is outrageously high in omega-6 whereas 100 percent grass-fed organic beef has the beautiful balance of omega-6 and 3 that God intended. In fact, the fat from grass-fed beef is extremely healthful whereas the fat of commercial beef is the reason people are getting cancer.

Several of the recipes in this book suggest the use of animal fats. Tallow, fat, or lard is an excellent medium as long as it was rendered from *pastured* beef, chicken, or pork. It can take the heat and it tastes good. My section about bone broth and rendering fats follows.

If there is no problem with anyone in the family having milk products, real butter is highly recommended, provided it is *pastured* butter (again, to avoid the animal products derived from animals which have been fed GMO grains). Melted dairy-free butter can be used. This, however, is usually soy, which can be a problem for some (and is definitely off the menu during elimination diet). It should definitely be the kind made with *organic* soy.

## Bone Broth and Rendered Animal Fats

What's the big deal about bone broth? This is probably the cheapest good thing you can have which helps to heal your gut.

A good broth can be made from any single type of meat or poultry or you can mix different bones from say chicken, beef and pork. Of course, I make plain chicken or beef broth but sometimes I make broth from a mix of chicken and beef or chicken and pork bones, if I can find good pork. By good pork, I mean organic or from a reputable local farm which has pastured animals but may not have the "organic" designation. It is very important that you always use organic or grass-fed chicken, beef, or pork bones, not commercially raised animals. It matters that the animals are not fed GMO grains.

Mixing the bones became a thing when I discovered that our cat would only have the mixture instead of plain chicken broth or beef broth. Likely, it was simply that the mixed one was cooked longer and, thus, was better bone broth. The longer you cook the bones the better it is. The cat clearly prefers that the broth be cooked longer. Since I have discovered this treat for our elderly cat, he has not been throwing up nearly as much. I know you really wanted to read that! But seriously, I knew it would do him some good and that unpleasant symptom crops up more when I have not had any on hand to give him. Go figure.

I do keep some bulk store-bought quarts of organic chicken broth for larger recipes and soups. However, if you cannot find organic chicken broth without gluten contaminants you will have to make your own. Chicken broth is made by simply simmering everything left after a roasted chicken has been served. That means, the skin, fat, bones, and gristle are submerged in a big pot of water, brought to a boil and then cooked for a long time with the heat lowered. Cover the pot and keep the simmer very low and you will not have to add much water. You will have very good chicken broth or "stock" in just a few hours but bone broth is cooked for at least twenty-four hours. Just turn it off when you go to bed and back on when you wake up. Obviously you must add water at times when the level lowers. I imagine that this can also be done in a slow cooker or a pressure cooker, but I have no idea how long it should be in these appliances. Once in a while I make gravy (which is just broth thickened with corn starch or rice flour) but most commonly I use this broth for soups and for adding liquid and flavor in cooking. Although I cannot interest anyone else in the family, I enjoy a warm cup of it with a scoop of collagen dissolved in it and a dash of salt and pepper before I go to bed. It's like a healing double dose not only for healthy hair and skin, but more importantly, for all my connective tissues and bones (not to mention my digestive system!)

I have found that my natural foods store has beef bones from local farms in the freezer. They are sold as "soup bones" and usually do have a small amount of meat on them which can be removed after a couple of hours of cooking and set aside in the refrigerator if you want to make soup later or just eat it. Again, the longer you simmer it the more collagen and amino acids will end up in the broth.

You will also find that the natural food store has bone broth in the freezer or the refrigerator. But this comes at quite a price, in my opinion, when it's very easy to make a whole lot of your own very good bone broth and put it into smaller containers for the freezer.

This brings me to the subject of rendered animal fats. You might be asking why a person would want animal fat. It does not burn easily or change structure when it is used to sauté vegetables. As it comes from good organic animals, it is a "good fat" and it is really the best to begin the process of browning your meat that you are about to roast. In order to render fat, after you have made your bone broth as above, and you've strained it and cooled it enough to refrigerate, refrigerate it. The fat rises to the surface and is easily removed to a small container. Use this within a week or freeze it. It will probably have some particles that went through the strainer and also some trace amount of broth. Often I save up the fat in the freezer, and then I will put it all together in a **saucepan** on the stove or a **microwaveable container** and heat it well with a plate over it. I fold a **strong paper towel** into a sort of funnel (but without the hole at the bottom) or use a **coffee filter** like an extra fine sieve for the fat to go into a **jelly jar or other heat-safe coverable container**. As it cools it will be harder for it to continue through the fibers so you may put some in, wait for it to drain and then you may have to reheat the fat you still have to filter to keep it all going through. Now it will be beautifully filtered and easily accessible. It will keep well for some weeks in the refrigerator—just that the very small amount of broth at the bottom will mold pretty quickly after it is exposed to the air. Probably a safer storage would be smaller containers that only hold a few tablespoons and can be frozen until you want to use each one.

**Note**: Whether you save rendered fat or not it is important to *never* let it go down the drain. At room temperature animal fats will congeal and they harden at just a little cooler temperature. Thus, if they go into the sewer system they can be a big problem. So when cleaning your broiler pan after cooking meat, use paper towels or carefully scrape to remove fat to the trash before you wash the pan.

For the Adventurous Fish-Lover

A very good fish broth can be made when shrimp shells are boiled. Of course, I only do this with good wild-caught shrimp because the farm-raised shrimp are being fed GMO grains and may also be subject to polluting run-off. So when you've found some beautiful wild-caught shrimp for your dinner, don't hate the long boring job of peeling them before you can cook them. Instead, think about your delicious seafood soup you will make later after you have simmered the shells for 1–2 hours. Of course, you can also put it into the freezer until you are ready to make soup.

# How to Cook Vegetables

My parents enjoy their food very plain. Even though I do more to make vegetables interesting, I appreciate their example. My mother always had at least one cooked vegetable *and* a salad at dinner. She would do a second cooked vegetable if she knew some of us would not take the other one. And for my entire childhood, I hated cooked cauliflower but loved it raw and I ate it. If your family will not eat their vegetables I suggest that you take this very seriously and get them interested. I do *not* suggest you start with frozen vegetables (except peas) because they will not taste good. Fresh vegetables are different. If after great effort you really cannot get them to eat any of these cooked, I suggest you cut raw vegetables—beyond the lettuce and cucumber of a salad. The more colors, the better!

## Broccoli, Cauliflower, String Beans, and Zucchini or Yellow Squash

They each have different cooking times but my method is the same. Wash and cut said vegetable to reasonable sizes for eating (not too small). Load a **medium saucepan** with about 2–3 cups of the vegetable. This will be plenty for dinner. Put about 1½ inches of water in the bottom. Cover and put on to boil 10–15 minutes before you want to serve dinner. After it has been steaming for a few minutes check doneness with a **fork**. Do not let the water all boil away. It will ruin your vegetables and your pan too! Different times for different vegetables: I like any of these to be cooked but not mushy. It is up to you how you want them. Probably more nutrition is retained in them the less you cook them. The same method can be used to cook them from frozen. Frozen vegetables save the time to wash and cut but fresh is always better.

## Serving Suggestions

For cauliflower, my own favorite is just salt and fresh ground pepper. The Italians in our family all like to add olive oil and vinegar.

Broccoli might be served similarly to cauliflower, but our family prefers a good balsamic salad dressing or just plain tamari. For those who can still use dairy although it is more caloric, I highly recommend the ranch dressing made from yogurt in the refrigerated area of grocery store. Of course, always be checking labels!

Mom and Dad have always used butter, salt and pepper on their squash, which is also loved in our family with the adjustment of DF butter. Whatever you can do to get everyone to eat his or her vegetables, do it.

String beans can be enjoyed any of these ways. Hopefully you've cooked enough to have some left after dinner. Chilled in the fridge, they are an incredibly delicious inoffensive vegetable for a lunchbox using my Tamari-Ginger Dressing. I do not suggest you put any cruciferous vegetables in lunchboxes to avoid any embarrassment at school upon their opening!

## Beets: several ways to cook them

No matter what you do, beets take a long time to cook. Many people have never even tried fresh beets but have only had them pickled from a can usually at a salad bar. I invite you to try them fresh cooked. By far, the easiest and quickest way to cook beets is in a **pressure cooker**. My mother has always done it this way to this day. She just trims the root end and the gnarly top and cuts them to a consistent size—maybe quarters, but it depends on how large the beets are. She and my dad also enjoy the tops, which are called beet greens even though they are red stalks. I never acquired the taste for this part. She has always left the whole cooker in the sink after dowsing the closed top with cold water after the proper time of cooking has been reached to "temper" them. We are talking about a regular pressure cooker that goes on the stove, not one of the new ones that plug in. After this few minutes resting in the sink, she is then able to remove the skins just before they get to the table (or we can remove them ourselves). I have done the same for years until something happened to the seal on my pressure cooker.

One can roast them with olive oil, salt, and pepper in a hot oven like 425° starting with 30 minutes. They can take at least as long as potatoes. It depends on the size of the pieces. I used to laboriously peel them before doing this and found that they are delicious this way but they tend to be a bit dried out. One day my niece (who had never tried fresh beets) exclaimed that they tasted like potatoes (I do like a lot of butter and salt and pepper on them) and that made me think of them more like potatoes (although they are no relation) and I suddenly thought that there was really no good reason why one had to peel a beet.

Later I began to cook them in the microwave in a **covered casserole dish** with about ½ a cup of water. I scrub the skin, pare off the root end and the gnarly top end and roughly cut them just like Mom but now I don't bother removing the skin after the cooking. It may take several bouts of cooking ten minutes at a time. In between you have to stir them and test them to see if a fork will go in. Another way to cook them if you do not have a microwave is the same preparation with the casserole dish in the oven at 350°. After 40 minutes, remove them, turn them to the other side, recover and put them back in the oven for 20 minutes. They might still not be done. If the water is almost gone add another third or half cup more hot water and put them back in for another 20 minutes. I know, it is really a long time without a pressure cooker! But they are so much better than canned.

## Brussels Sprouts

These take a long time and Mom uses the pressure cooker. Actually she pressure cooks just about every vegetable. I prefer these roasted. Use an open **casserole dish**, clean (remove any loose outer leaves) and cut them in half, toss with olive oil, salt, and pepper. Roast at 375° for 20 minutes. Remove and stir them. Roast another 15–20 minutes. They should be tender but slightly firm in the middle. Some people like to add balsamic vinegar to the whole thing before roasting.

## Roasted Vegetables

Use root vegetables, onions and potatoes as well as broccoli and cauliflower prepared as Brussels sprouts above. Add some Brussels sprouts, too! If you want to put some tenderer vegetables like summer squashes and green beans, put them in after the first 20–30 minutes passes, toss them with the selection you have already started and then continue roasting as above.

## Spinach Three Ways

To me, there are two kinds of spinach. Full-grown and baby. Again, the process for full-grown spinach comes from my dear mother. The great thing is that you don't have to wash it because it happens in the cooking. Put a **very large pot** of water on to boil. When it is boiling, drop in your spinach and move it around with a **slotted spoon**. After only about 1–2 minutes lift the spinach leaves out onto your serving dish. The sand should be left in the bottom of the pot of water. When my children were very young I used to then chop it up, removing the stalks before adding a little tamari sauce. They loved it!

Baby spinach is already triple-washed so I dump it into a **medium-sized microwave-able bowl**. Get as much as you can fit into it. Add 2 T. water, put a **plate** over the top, and microwave 2 minutes. Be careful getting it out and because everything is very hot. Protecting yourself with **potholders**, hold the plate edge to the edge of the bowl away from you and tip it until the water drains out into the sink. Or if this is too difficult just plop the spinach into a **strainer** over the sink. Quickly dump it back into the hot bowl, sprinkle with tamari sauce, and mix it with a **fork**. Serve immediately.

This third way to cook spinach is more of a recipe but it is incredibly delicious and can be eaten while on the elimination diet.

Ingredients:
1 lb. triple-washed spinach
3–5 fresh cloves of garlic, chopped to under ⅜"
6 T. EVOO
sea salt

After chopping the garlic divide it into two portions.

In a **large heavy pot** warm 3 T. of EVOO over medium heat and add one portion of garlic and sprinkle liberally with sea salt. With a **spoon** or **spatula** keep moving the garlic to that it never burns. Let it cook slowly and when a couple of pieces have just begun to brown slightly add half of the spinach. Move the spinach around to both coat it with the garlic olive oil and cook all the leaves evenly. When they are uniform keep stirring for about 30 seconds and then remove the spinach to a **serving dish**. Remove any juices from the pot and repeat the whole process with the remaining ingredients.

## Mushrooms

Shitaki, maitaki, oyster, bunashimeji (beech mushrooms), crimini, and white mushrooms just to name a few...did I mention that we live in the area that is the mushroom capital of the world? Ethan recently began liking them but Nina has loved mushrooms since she could pick up her food with her fingers. A quick rinse, and then I remove the whole stem of shitake mushrooms or just cut off the dried end of the stems of the white or crimini types and then slice the caps. With the cluster types, I remove some of the bottom of the stems and then split them so that they will cook evenly. Just a little olive oil in a **frying pan**, and then toss them into the oil when it's hot. Do not overcrowd the pan or they might become soggy—they have a lot of moisture. After a moment add a little salt and pepper. Do not let the heat get too high but fry them until they are nicely browned in places. Delicious on a salad or with a steak—or anything!

# Soups

## Potato Leek Soup

Ingredients:
2 T. DF butter (or real butter if dairy not a problem)
3–4 leeks, white part only, finely chopped
1 medium onion, small dice
4–5 medium potatoes, peeled and large diced
4 c. chicken broth
salt and pepper
chives, chopped (optional to garnish)
1 c. cream (optional, if dairy is not a problem)

* In your **stockpot**, sauté the leeks and onion in the butter for about 3 minutes.
* Add the potatoes and broth, cover and simmer for about 15 minutes or until the potatoes are soft.
* Put everything into a **whole food processor** or **blender** and puree.

This is delicious comfort food as is.
If you add the cream it becomes Vichyssoise, which can be served hot or ice cold.
Garnish with chives if desired.

*Butternut Squash and Bean Soup*

## Butternut Squash and Bean Soup

This is another fantastic comfort food.

Ingredients:
2 thick slices of bacon (preferably uncured meaning no nitrates) OR
2 T. reserved bacon grease from having cooked such bacon as above or if you do not desire to
    have the smoked bacon flavor, 2 T. of butter or dairy-free butter may be used
1 ½ c. (about 1 medium) onion, chopped
6 garlic cloves, minced or pressed
3–4 c. chicken broth
4 c. cooked butternut squash (see how to cook fresh squash in the dessert section before
    Pumpkin or Squash Puddings—and this can be done the night or day before and
    refrigerated.)
2 15 oz. cans cannellini beans
1 15 oz. can diced tomatoes
1 t. chopped fresh rosemary (use a little more if it is dried)
salt and pepper

✳ If starting from bacon, sauté the bacon in a **large heavy pot** until crispy and remove the bacon. Otherwise, warm the 2 T. bacon grease or butter in the pot to medium.

✳ Add onion and garlic to the bacon grease or butter. Sauté for about 8–10 minutes, not too hot because you don't want to burn the garlic.

✳ In a **whole food processor** or **blender**, blend the squash, onion and garlic, chicken broth, beans and rosemary until smooth. (This may have to be done in a few stages if the machine is not big enough for everything together, in which case you should put the onion/garlic mixture into the first one so that you can start putting everything back into the stockpot.)

✳ After all of the pureed ingredient are in the stockpot, add the diced tomatoes, bring it all to a boil and then lower the heat. Simmer the soup for about 15 minutes stirring frequently to keep it from sticking.

✳ Salt and fresh ground pepper to taste.

## Onion Soup
Elimination diet friendly

Ingredients:
3–4 onions
1 T. beef tallow (fat)
3–4 c. beef bone broth
salt and fresh ground pepper to taste

✳ After removing the dry layers and any rough outer layer and the stem end of each onion slice them thinly however you want them to appear in the soup.

✳ In a **large saucepan** heat beef tallow and when hot add the onions. Stir and sauté them until they are tender and glossy.

✳ Add the beef broth, bring the soup to a boil, and reduce the heat. Simmer for 10–15 minutes. Salt and Pepper to taste.

This is really a French onion soup base. The problem is that no gluten-free bread will hold up to being set in the bottom of the bowl so I do *not* suggest that. If you wanted to bake it in some oven-safe dishes to melt cheese on the top (like Fontina or mozzarella) go for it if you can take dairy. Be careful. Use a tray. Adding dairy negates its elimination diet friendliness.

## Cod Fish Soup with Mustard and Singapore Seasoning

The mustard and seasoning make this seafood soup into something exotic and fresh tasting!

Ingredients:
4 c. seafood broth (you buy or make ahead using my instructions at the end of the broth section above)
1 c. celery, chopped
1 c. carrots, medium dice
2 c. Shanghai cabbage (although it is wrong, it is more commonly called baby bok choy) OR bok choy or mustard greens, chopped and rinsed well, but if none of these are available you can use baby spinach at the end.
1 c. frozen peas
1 c. green onions, chopped
2 T. Chinese cooking wine
2 T. tamari sauce

1 T. dry mustard (Chinese is best)

1 t. Singapore seasoning (contains black pepper, garlic, onion, turmeric, coriander, cumin, fenugreek, ginger, nutmeg, fennel, cinnamon, white pepper, cardamom, clove, and cayenne red pepper)

½–¾ lb. cod, cut into 1–2" pieces

* In your **stockpot**, bring to a boil, reduce the heat and simmer the seafood broth, celery, and carrots for 10 minutes.
* Add the cabbage or greens (if using spinach, add it with the peas having skipped this step) Cook 5 minutes.
* Add the peas and cook 1 minute.
* Add the green onions, wine and tamari, mustard and seasoning, cook 1 minute.
* Add the fish and cook just until done—maybe 1–2 minutes. It will begin to fall apart but take it off the heat before the fish becomes tough.
* Serve immediately.

*Tamarind Seafood Soup.*

## Tamarind Seafood Soup
### (Includes elimination diet adjustment)

Wet tamarind is found among Mexican or Asian foods but this soup is decidedly Asian. It adds a tangy—almost like tomato but not—flavor changing the straight fish flavor of the broth. It is very easy to make.

Ingredients:
3 T. seedless wet tamarind
1 c. boiled water (can be done in a mug in the microwave if desired)
1 c. celery
1 c. carrot
1 T. peanut oil (EVOO if on elimination diet)
6 Shanghai cabbages (see description in Cod Fish Soup above)
4–6 scallions
3–4 c. seafood broth
1 c. frozen cold water shrimp
1 c. small frozen scallops or angostinos
1–2 T. tamari sauce (use ½ t. salt instead and no pepper sauce for elimination diet)
Thai pepper sauce (optional but highly recommended)
fresh chopped cilantro (optional)

* In a medium saucepan begin warming the seafood broth.
* Pour the boiled water into a **mug** and mash and break up the tamarind into it with a **fork**. Set aside while you chop the celery and carrots.
* In another **pan** at least four-quart size, heat the peanut or EVO oil. Add the celery and carrots and stir until they are sizzling. Add ½ c. water and cover.
* Remove any yellowed leaves or edges, cut the bottom end off and rinse the Shanghai cabbage thoroughly. You may have to keep rinsing towards the middles as you cut them apart. Chop and add the white parts to the pot, saving the chopped green parts to add later.
* Do not let the water in the vegetables boil away before you add the seafood broth. Take it off the stove if it is gone before your broth is heated through.
* Add the warmed seafood broth to the vegetables and bring it to a boil. Turn it down again.

* By scraping it through a strainer with a spoon, add the tamarind mash. Much of it will remain in the strainer too big to go through. That's good. Scrape only the underside of the strainer into the soup.
* Let it simmer as you clean and chop the scallions.
* Add frozen seafood, cabbage greens, scallions, bring it back up to a boil and reduce the heat again.
* Add tamari to taste.
* Add Thai pepper sauce to taste.
* Serve immediately with some fresh cilantro sprinkled on top if desired.

# Sides, Salads, and Snacks

## Sautéed Baby Kale
### (E-Diet Friendly)

This is a good general way to cook any course greens (including fully-grown chopped kale).

11 oz. baby kale
2 shallots, sliced
3 cloves garlic, minced or pressed
2 T. avocado oil
chicken broth (maybe up to 1 c. )
¼ c. Chinese cooking wine or sherry
¼–½ tsp. sea salt
1 tsp. sugar or honey (this small amount is probably okay but you can leave it out if you are
 feeling virginal on your elimination diet).

* In a **large frying pan** over medium heat sauté the shallots in the oil 1–2 minutes and
  then add the garlic. After another minute add enough chicken broth to stop the sizzle
  and then the wine, salt, and sugar.
* When everything is combined add the kale. Keep simmering it adding chicken broth
  from time to time until it is consistently cooked.
* Serve after most of the liquid is gone.

## Rosemary Roasted Sweet Potatoes
(E-diet friendly)

This recipe can also be used for regular potatoes or we recommend a mix of both sweet potatoes and potatoes but, or course these variations are not e-diet friendly.

✳ Preheat oven to 375º.

Ingredients:
5–6 medium sized sweet potatoes (not related to the potato)
3–4 T. EVOO
1–2 T. dried rosemary
½–1 t. salt
½ t. fresh ground pepper

✳ Peel and cut sweet potatoes into about 1–2" × 1" × ¾" or like steak fries or any way that will be a consistent size.
✳ Toss all the potatoes in a good-sized **bowl** with the oil and seasonings.
✳ When well mixed, spread them in a **roasting pan** in one layer.
✳ Bake 15 minutes.
✳ Remove the pan and quickly scrap and turn them so that they are not stuck to the pan.
✳ Bake for another 15–20 minutes.
✳ If they have not dried enough they may be overly mushy in which case you should stir them and return them to the oven for more cooking. Keep watching. Sometimes they never get crispy but they still taste amazing. Other times they come out just the way you hoped. I think it has a lot to do with how much moisture the potatoes have.

## Roasted Green Tomatoes
(Gluten-free, dairy-free)

I plant a lot of tomatoes. By the middle of the season I have so many it is hard to use them all (unless I make sauce or soup, but that makes so little out of so many!). I have found I can preserve these roasted green tomatoes in the freezer when a ton are coming in the beginning or just before the frost and they must be picked green. Green tomatoes can sometimes be found in the grocery store and at farm markets. These seasoned slabs of tomato make a wonderful layer for lasagna or even reheated as a tangy vegetable alongside a rustic main course.

Large—and medium-sized green tomatoes
duck fat (best, if you have it, but you could use chicken fat instead)
sea salt
fresh ground pepper

* Preheat oven to 425°.
* Slice tomatoes crosswise to the stem end into slabs about ⅜" wide.
* In a **9"×13" baking dish** spread a little less than a tablespoon of fat around on the whole bottom of dish.
* Cover the bottom of the dish with a single layer of tomatoes, edge-to-edge.
* Salt and pepper them.
* Roast them for 8–10 minutes. Carefully turn them over and roast them again 8–10 minutes. They will be a little tender but still quite firm.
* Lay them on a **plate** to cool.
* Repeat this process until all your tomato slabs are roasted. You may have to drain out the juice before each new batch and before you add a little more fat to cover the bottom.
* To freeze, lay them on **parchment paper** with parchment between the layers of tomatoes in the container you will freeze. This way they can easily be removed in frozen state when you are ready to layer your lasagna.

## Curried Collards and Potatoes

This is my daughter's and my favorite way to eat collards and I always make it when my vegetarian sister comes or we go there to visit.

Ingredients:
5 medium potatoes, peeled, and cut into biggish bite-sized pieces

1–2 bunches of collards
3–4 T. DF butter (or regular butter if dairy is not a problem)
½ t. whole black or brown mustard seeds
1 medium onion, small dice
2 cloves garlic, minced or pressed
¼ t. curry
½ t. garam masala
½ t. turmeric
salt to taste

＊ In a **large pot** of water, bring the potatoes to a boil and cook for about 10 minutes. They should be tender but not too soft. Drain, rinse in cold water, drain again and set aside. This can be done ahead and refrigerated until use. I recommend it because it does reduce the time it takes to create this excellent dish.

＊ Rinse the collards well, remove stems and veins all the way until the vein disappears, and then chop into 1-inch strips about 2–3 inches in length.

＊ In a **heavy skillet**, heat the butter to medium and add the mustard seed. Stir and then add the onion, garlic, and the rest of the spices with a little salt. Stir for a minute or two.

＊ Add the collards, mixing and turning them. I like to use a **spoon** and a **spatula** because there is so much greenery that it wants to jump out of the pan!

＊ When the collards have wilted add the potatoes and keep stirring until you see that all the potatoes are yellow. Cover and cook them for a couple more minutes. If you don't have a cover to fit the pan it does not really matter. Just keep it moving and get it heated through. Add more salt if desired.

## Latkes
(Gluten—and grain-free, dairy-free)

One of the very few things that I actually fry once in a while, my kids and Steve love these at breakfast, lunch or dinner! Ethan likes some DF sour cream or ketchup and Nina loves them with apple sauce (of which you could open your *own* jar if you follow my recipe for apple sauce)

Ingredients:
5 medium potatoes
½–¾ c. green onion, chopped fine to small
1 t. sugar

½ t. sea salt

¼ t. fresh ground pepper

avocado oil

chicken fat (although chicken fat is traditional and delicious, you could use coconut oil or just more avocado oil instead)

* Chop the green onion first so the grated potato does not turn brown while you are doing this.
* Wash, peel and grate the potatoes into a **9"×13" pan** with a potholder or pad under one end to make the juice drain away from grated potato. Squeeze some more juice out and remove either the juice or the potato to a different bowl.
* Quickly mix in the onion, sugar, salt and pepper.
* Heat **large frying pan** medium-high with about 3 T. chicken fat and 3 T. avocado oil.
* Clump and flatten small amounts in your hands and drop into the hot oils. Keep them ½ inch or thinner. You will get used to what to do after a couple. Do not move them for about 3 minutes while they brown on the bottom. It might take longer than that.
* While you wait prepare a **plate** with a couple layers of **paper towel**.
* With a **thin spatula** scoop and turn them over carefully. They should be nicely browned and crispy around the edges. Fry about 3 more minutes for that side to be the same color. Remove and place on paper towels.
* Add about 2–3 T. each of chicken fat and avocado oil before each batch. Repeat until all done layering them with more paper towels on the plate. Although they are greasy, they are a special treat once in a while.

## Apple Sauce
### (Elimination diet friendly)

Ingredients:

5–10 lbs. apples, choose at least two types (organic)

2 T.–¼ c. sugar

cinnamon

fresh ground nutmeg (already ground is okay but fresh is excellent)

* Quarter or roughly cut the apples—don't even bother to core them.
* Fill a **large heavy pot** with however many you want and add water until you see it come to just below the top layer of apples. Bring to a boil uncovered.

✳ Reduce heat to a good bubbling simmer and cook until they are all quite soft stirring occasionally to mix the top ones down.

✳ Over a **large bowl**, put them through a **strainer** using the edge of a **large spoon** to scrape. Better yet is the **Foley food mill**. I have always had one (thanks, Mom!). I even wore out the one she gave me and had to find another. This timeless contraption is so excellent for exactly this job, but also for making your own tomato sauce and milling freshly cooked pumpkin or squash.

✳ When you have done the best you can to extract the liquid and pulp, discard skin and core refuse that is left. Pour the apple sauce back into the pot and heat on medium-low.

✳ When is has reduced and thickened add a small amount of cinnamon and nutmeg (like half as much nutmeg as cinnamon…I always think less is more because these spices can overpower so use your judgement)

✳ Add some sugar—not too much at first because oversweet is terrible. Adjust it to your taste (not for elimination diet).

✳ Serve it hot or warm (great to top with a little heavy cream or coconut whip on each serving as a dessert).

Or you can serve it cold from the fridge.
It goes well with a turkey or pork dinner and/or, of course, the latkes!

## Homemade Stuffing
(Gluten-free, dairy-free)

Ingredients:
3–4 loaves gluten-free bread
1 shallot, minced
2 stalks of celery, minced
1½ c. chicken broth
6 T. DF butter
2–3 cloves garlic, pressed
2 T. fresh parsley, minced

Herb mix:
1½ t. salt
½ t. fresh ground pepper
1 t. oregano
1 t. marjoram

* Buy several different kinds of gluten-free bread. Avoid the "soft" types. I used a honey white, a 7-grain, a seeded 10-grain, and a package of sourdough deli slices (look in both the freezer section and the shelf-stable section of the grocery store).
* Cut slices into small cubes no larger than ½", enough to fill **two half sheet pans or cookie sheets** with slightly more than a single layer. I found that the "dehydrate" setting nowhere near did the job. So finally, late at night I set the oven to "bake" at 170 with both sheets in it and went to bed! Early in the morning they were perfectly desiccated. Maybe you don't want to leave your oven going all night and maybe it does not go as low as 170. You may be able to do it at 200 but watch it and stir it around occasionally—you do not want to burn all your expensive bread.
* Set oven to 325°.
* Measure 7 c. of dried bread into a **large bowl**. You may have some extra which you can close airtight in a bag for use at another time. But do not just add it in because these measurements are the right balance of wet, dry, and butter for great stuffing.
* In a **microwave safe bowl** or **saucepan** heat the chicken broth and butter just to about boiling and then remove from microwave or burner.
* Sauté the shallot and celery.
* When this mixture is softened (cooked) add the garlic and sauté for about 30 seconds more.
* Add the vegetables to the broth mixture.
* Add the parsley and 2 t. of herb mix and mix well.
* Toss the warm liquid mixture with the bread in the bowl. Toss and mix well two more times within 5 minutes.
* Fill a **9"×13" oven dish** with the stuffing, cover with foil, and bake it for 25 minutes.

It is good at this point or you can refrigerate it when it has cooled until use within a couple of days. Just reheat it covered for about 30 minutes.

*Korean-Style Noodles*

## Korean-Style Noodles
(Contains soy, sesame, and peanut oils)

Before we went gluten-free we had discovered this wonderful dish made daily for lunch at the Korean grocery store. I *had* to recreate it gluten-free!

Ingredients:
1 lb. sweet potato noodles, spaghetti shaped, not linguini shaped
2 c. red onion, sliced
2 c. red bell pepper, sliced
12 oz. baby spinach
10 oz. shitake mushrooms (before the stems are removed)
1–2 T. peanut oil (or avocado oil)
2 T. sesame oil
2–3 T. tamari sauce
sea salt (optional)

* First put a **large pot** of water on to boil. The noodles will take only about 5–6 minutes to cook, so wait until you have begun to cook the vegetables before you put the noodles into your boiling water.
* Cut the onion(s) in half, top to bottom, and slice the same direction to get thin sliver shaped pieces.
* Cut the red bell pepper similarly to get long thin pieces.
* Remove the stems from the shitake mushrooms (discard) and then slice the tops into thin strips.
* In a **large skillet** pour some peanut oil, wait for the temperature to be medium—not too hot, and add the onions. They should sizzle a little but do not let them brown. After about 2–3 minutes add the peppers. I like to season each of the vegetables as they go in with a small amount of sea salt but you can do without it if you wish.
* When the peppers are slightly tender, add the mushrooms. Sauté for about 2 minutes.
* Add the spinach in big handfuls. I use **two bamboo spatulas** to turn and stir in the spinach to incorporate all the vegetables evenly. When all the spinach is wilted evenly (but not overcooked) turn off the heat.
* When the noodles are cooked and drained, put the sesame oil into the pot in which they were cooked and toss them back into it to keep them from sticking together. I find that these noodles are too long to mix easily so I cut them a few times with a pair of **kitchen shears or clean scissors**.

✳ Add the tamari sauce to the vegetables and then toss everything together in the big pot. Taste and adjust if you think more tamari or sesame is needed. Voila!

## Lotus Root Kinpo
(Contains peanut oil soy)

I always feel so good when I eat this. Burdock root is really good for you and everything else is healthy too! Burdock and lotus root are usually available in your Asian grocery store as are the dried mushrooms. You can the omit lotus root if you are unable to find any.

Ingredients:
1–2 T. peanut oil
1½ c. burdock root (10" section peeled and julienned)
1 ¾ c. carrots (about 2 big carrots, peeled and julienned)
6–7 dried shitake mushrooms (or 1 ½ c. if they are already sliced)
12–14 slices of lotus root
1 ½" cube of ginger, minced
2–3 cloves of garlic, minced
2 T. Chinese cooking wine
2 T. tamari sauce
5 green onions

✳ In a **medium bowl** soak the lotus root in 3 c. water for about 1 hour. This is about how long it will take to cut the burdock and carrots. About ½ way through this time add the mushrooms to the water to be soaked 20–30 minutes.
✳ Cut the burdock root and carrots. Set aside.
✳ Remove the lotus from the water and cut the pieces each into six pie pieces. Set aside.
✳ Gently squeeze the water from the mushrooms, reserving the water. Slice the mushrooms (removing any stalks) narrowly or small dice.
✳ Heat **skillet** and add peanut oil, then the lotus, garlic and ginger. This is another recipe for which I like to use **two cooking implements** because all the flat sides of the vegetables want to slide against the bottom of the pan instead of turning. Stir for a few seconds, and then add the burdock and carrots, incorporating everything consistently.
✳ Add ½–¾ c. of the mushroom water and the wine. Stirring occasionally, let it cook while you clean and chop the green onions into narrow diagonal slices. Stir occasionally.

Note:

If the burdock and carrots are still quite hard before the addition of green onion, first add a little more mushroom water and cook it down again before adding the onions.

＊ When the moisture is almost cooked away add the onions and mushrooms. Quickly incorporate and add the tamari. Stir it in, cook for 2 more minutes and taste it. Add more tamari if needed.

## Salmon Egg Salad
(Contains egg elimination diet adjustment below)

This is a little more elegant than tuna salad but just as easy to prepare! I actually had two hard-boiled eggs in the fridge and about 7 oz of salmon when I did this the first time.

Ingredients:
6–8 oz. cold cooked salmon
2 hard-boiled eggs
1 dill pickle, finely chopped
½–¾ c. celery, finely chopped
2 T. organic mayonaise
1–2 T. Dijon mustard
¼ t. paprika
⅛ t. sea salt
⅛ t. garlic powder
fresh ground pepper

Mix everything except the last ingredient together and then grind the pepper to your taste. I love to eat this with lentil chips, but you could fill stalks of celery with it or wrap it up in Romaine or iceberg lettuce leaves.

You can make this e-diet friendly by leaving out the egg, mayo and paprika and adding a tablespoon of extra virgin olive oil. I guarantee that this will still be a delicious and satisfying treat!

**Note:** Whenever I make egg salad of any sort, I always remove the yolks and mix them well with the mayonnaise and seasonings first so that it is smooth. It also makes it easier to cut or mash the whites uniformly. Maybe it makes absolutely no difference to you!

## Shrimp and Avocado Salad
(Elimination diet friendly)

Ingredients:
5–8 cold cooked shrimp, depending on how large they are (and how hungry you are!)
2 c. chopped Romaine lettuce
half an avocado, sliced
1–2 T. fresh lemon juice
1–2 T. EVOO
sea salt and fresh ground pepper to taste

Fresh, filling, and full of everything you need!

## Chicken-Artichoke Salad
(Elimination diet friendly)

Ingredients:
cooked chicken
large jar of preserved artichokes
celery
green onion

This can be made any size depending how much prepared chicken you have.

＊ Have your chicken cooked, cold, and chopped or shredded as you please.
＊ Mix together the same amount of chopped preserved artichokes as you have prepared chicken and add a teaspoon of the oil from the top of the jar of artichokes.
＊ Chop finely the green onion and celery which together amount to about half of the amount of chicken.
＊ Close the lid of the artichoke jar very tightly and turn it over and shake it until the flavorful vinegar mixture is completely combined with the oil. Pour on 2 tablespoons over the salad and mix well.

This doesn't need anything and would be great with a handful of sweet potato chips!

## Chicken Salad
(Contains egg)

Ingredients:
2 c. cooked chicken, cold, and chopped or shredded
¾–1 c. celery, finely chopped
¾–1 c. green onion, finely chopped
2 T. mayonnaise
1–2 T. Dijon mustard
1 T. fresh lemon juice
1 T. white wine vinegar
salt and fresh ground pepper to taste

*Italian Tomato Salad*

## Italian Tomato Salad

I learned this from my mother-in-law having it with every Sunday dinner. It is, of course, best done with summer tomatoes. Big pieces of fresh garlic that are easy to avoid eating flavor the oil and thus, the tomatoes. After dinner, if any was left, she always removed the garlic pieces before storing tomato salad in the refrigerator. She always said that it would be too strong the next day. When I do this, sometimes I keep this garlic separately in the fridge to be cooked soon into a marinara sauce or some type of stir fry.

Ingredients:
4–6 medium to large summer tomatoes (or the best ones you can find in the store)
4 cloves of fresh garlic, roughly cut
6 leaves of fresh basil (or more!)
4 T. EVOO
salt to taste

* Quarter the tomatoes or cut them on the large side. Lay them in a **low serving bowl**. She always had them in a single layer.
* Add the garlic around.
* Cut the basil into thin strips and distribute it.
* I don't actually know how much olive oil really goes on because it is drizzled on liberally.

Note: You really cannot have too much oil on this dish. The Silvers always enjoyed it after the tomatoes were gone by dipping bread into it. Now that we are gluten-free, the bread should be toasted—or save the oil with the garlic to be used as I mentioned above—or it could go in a soup!

## Tomato and Cucumber Salad

I love this one in the summer—or any time of year. It is refreshing.

Ingredients:
1 cucumber, peeled and large diced
2–3 medium tomatoes, large diced
1 T. white wine vinegar
2 T. fresh squeezed lime juice
¼ t. dried oregano

¼ t. fresh ground pepper
⅛ t. salt

If you don't like oregano this salad is just as delicious without it—maybe add a tiny bit more pepper.

## Cucumber Salad

This was where the Tomato and Cucumber Salad got its start.

Ingredients:
2 cucumbers (about 3 cups, peeled and thinly cut)
1 small onion (about ¼ cup finely sliced)
2 T. white wine vinegar
1–2 T. water
¼ t. dried oregano
¼ t. fresh ground pepper
⅛ t. salt

## Asian Salad
### (Contains nuts)

1–2 servings soy
(spices & hot pepper sauce)

Ingredients:
2 c. chopped Romaine lettuce
½–¾ c. various chopped vegetables such as:
      carrots
      red bell pepper
      cucumber
      celery
⅛–¼ c. mix of curried cashews, coconut, pumpkin seeds, etc.
(I get this at my health food store—it even has candied ginger and raisins in it!) If you don't have a source, any curried nuts will do as long as there are no gluten ingredients

1 fresh mandarin or clementine, peeled and sectioned

Ingredients for dressing:
1 T. "Tamari Ginger Sauce"
1 T. toasted sesame oil
½ T. rice wine vinegar (optional)
dash of hot sauce (optional)

## Israeli Cabbage Salad
(Elimination diet friendly)

The secret is in how you slice the cabbage (the thinner the better). Ethan really loves this and calls it Purple Salad.

Ingredients:
¼ of a head of red cabbage
3–4 T. EVOO
¼–½ t. salt
1–2 T. white balsamic vinegar or white wine vinegar

As I said, it is the best to cut it very thinly and so that the shreds are not longer than 2 or 3 inches. I always remove the really thick parts but there is nothing wrong with including them.

After the long process of cutting, just toss all the ingredients together and enjoy with some Mediterranean style food, like hummus and chips, olives, and cucumber and tomato salad. Lamb!

Quinoa Salad here is made with red quinoa. Many people prefer white quinoa. Preparation is the same.

## Quinoa Salad
(A sort of tabbouleh)

1 c. quinoa
2 c. water
1 cucumber, peeled and finely chopped
4–5 green onions, finely chopped
5–6 sprigs Italian parsley, stalks removed and leaves minced (about 3 T.)
½ pint of grape tomatoes, quartered
½ a red, orange or yellow bell pepper, finely chopped
¼–½ c. lime juice (about 2 limes)
2 T. white wine vinegar
2 T. EVOO
¼ t. salt
fresh ground pepper

* In a **saucepan** bring water and quinoa to a boil, lower heat to simmer covered for about 15 minutes until the water is absorbed. Fluff with a **fork** and set it aside in a **small bowl** to cool.
* In another **small-medium bowl** mix together the rest of the salad ingredients.
* At this point, I like to chill both bowls and then finally combine it all so that the vegetables stay crisp.

**Notes on cutting the cucumber and green onions**: You can cut your cucumber any way you want, but I like the salad to have a nice overall small-sized consistency as the quinoa itself is a small grain. My way of cutting the cucumber after I have peeled it is to quarter it down the middle, each piece is then sliced down the middle again and then finely sliced across.

As for the green onions, after cutting off the root end, leaving most of the white part, I remove the tougher greens and the sinuous outer layer(s) leaving the tender greens. Slice them down the middle once or twice and then chop them finely (unless you prefer them to appear as little circles in your salad in which case you just slice them across whole)

## Pasta Salad with Black Beans

Be cutting the vegetables throughout the time it takes to boil the water, through the time the pasta and beans cook, and while the pasta and beans cool a little. This is really good right after it is done, still slightly warm.

121

Ingredients:
4 qts. water
1 8-oz. pkg. corn-quinoa rotini pasta
1 28-oz. can black beans, drained and rinsed
½ c. celery, finely chopped
½ c. green onion, finely chopped (about 4)
½ c. red bell pepper, finely chopped
2 c. fresh tomatoes, tiny dice, or quartered grape tomatoes
2 c. finely sliced cucumber
2 T. fresh basil, minced
2 T. EVOO
3–4 T. fresh squeezed lime juice (1–2 limes)
1 T. white wine vinegar
¼–½ t. fresh ground pepper
¼ t. salt

* Boil water in a **large pot**.
* Add the pasta and cook according to the package.
* In about the last minute of the pasta cooking, add the can of beans. Stir gently.
* When the pasta is done (test it—I find that it can take longer than the instructions say—it might be up to three minutes that the beans may cook with it) drain the pasta and beans in a **colander**, and then transfer them to a **large casserole dish** or **large bowl**.
* Drizzle 1 T. EVOO right away so that it does not stick. Gently mix it in. Wait about ten minutes before starting to mix in all the vegetables.
* When everything is cut and mixed in add the other tablespoon of olive oil, the lime juice, the vinegar, salt and pepper. Mix well. Serve or refrigerate immediately.

Note: You may want to add more vinegar, lime juice and/or salt to your taste. We love a lot of vinegar and lime. Salute!

## Puglia-Inspired Pasta

4 qts. Water
2 t. salt
1 8-oz. pkg. gluten-free pasta
¼ c. EVOO
3–4 cloves fresh garlic, just quarter each

1 lb. campari tomatoes, washed
2–3 c. arugula
fresh parmesan or manchego cheese, wide shavings (optional)

* Boil the water in a **large pot** with the salt.
* When the pasta goes into the water, in a **large frying pan or skillet** warm the olive oil over medium heat and add the garlic.
* Sprinkle a small pinch of salt, stir and cook the garlic for 1 minute.
* Add the tomatoes, stir and let cook 2–3 minutes until the tomatoes soften and turn off the stove.
* When the pasta is cooked and drained, add the arugula to the olive oil and tomatoes. Gently toss and turn to coat the leaves with oil.
* Add the pasta and incorporate gently so that the ingredients are uniformly mixed.
* Top with shaved cheese if using.

## Roasted Pecans

People are always putting sugar on their roasted nuts and I just want to say that the salty and slightly spicy perfection of these nuts is completely addictive! They are, of course, great on a salad, but I find them to be excellent car snacks and in-between meal pick-ups that really satisfy. Great as hors d'oeuvres, too!

Ingredients:
4 c. pecans
5–6 T. DF butter, melted
4 t. rosemary
1 t. salt
¼ t. cayenne
<¼ t. dried basil

* Set oven temperature to 325°.
* In a **large bowl** combine the melted butter, rosemary, salt, cayenne, and basil.
* Toss pecans in the mixture until they are well coated,
* Arrange on a **half-sheet pan** in a single layer.
* Bake for 10–12 minutes.

*Chewy Fruit and Nut Bonbons—homemade energy snacks!*

## Chewy Fruit and Nut Bonbons

I created these when I wanted to make something like a protein bar for Steve. They are a long process but they are a fantastic sweet snack. Even better would be if one were to make homemade marshmallows for that ingredient. I hear that it is really easy but I haven't yet tried it. In that case, the recipe would contain egg whites.

Makes about 60 bonbons.

**Small pastry (mini muffin) papers** are highly recommended because these treats will stick together.

Set oven to 350º.

Ingredients:
½–⅔ c. seeded and finely chopped dates (5 dates)
½ c. blond raisins
12 oz. (3 ¼ c.) walnuts
1½ c. hemp seeds (hearts—hulled)
25 marshmallows
3–4 T. DF butter
1 t. vanilla extract

* Chop whole walnuts roughly, place all but smallest pieces (about ½ c. including the dust) in a **medium bowl**. Set aside what is left.
* Add the chopped dates and raisins to the bowl of nuts.
* In a **½ sheet pan**, spread out the hemp seeds and roast at 350 for 10–13 minutes. Some lighter pans (cookie pans) may take only about 8 minutes. Do not let them burn.
* Toss reserved walnut pieces and dust with the hemp seeds.
* In a **large microwaveable bowl** place the marshmallows and DF butter.
* Heat in 30 second intervals, turning the bowl if necessary until melted. Mix well.
* Add vanilla.
* With a strong spoon stir in fruit and nuts. When incorporated, mix in ¾ c. of the hemp seed mixture.
* When the mixture is cooled but still pliable, drop by scant teaspoons into the seed mixture, roll and coat to make balls. Place each one into a pastry paper and then into a **cookie tin or other lidded container**. Cut a cardboard circle (or whatever shape your container is) to put in between the layers. They keep for a really long time.

## Spinach-Artichoke Dip

(Contains dairy or it can be adjusted to be dairy-free)

I love this recipe because it does not contain mayonnaise. It is a close approximation of a very well loved appetizer at a favorite restaurant that has the best gluten-free pizza crust made with chickpea flour. This recipe is great with any gluten-free crackers, chips, or even a toasted teff tortilla broken up.

Ingredients:
2 t. avocado or olive oil
1 c. onion, finely sliced
½ c. mushrooms, finely sliced
2 garlic cloves, pressed

16 oz. cream cheese, softened (DF sour cream)
½ c. sour cream or plain yogurt (DF ricotta or sour cream)
1 c. grated mozzarella cheese (DF mozzarella)
1 c. grated Parmesan cheese (refrigerated DF Parmesan—unless all you can find is the shaker
    DF Parmesan in which case, use only 1–2 T.)
14–20 oz. artichokes, drained and chopped coarsely
10–12 oz. of spinach, chopped coarsely
I like fresh baby spinach, but you can use frozen as long as you have thawed it and squeezed
    the water out of it before adding.
¼ t. fresh ground black pepper
¾ cup grated Fontina cheese (optional) (coconut gouda if you can get it)

* In a **small frying pan or sauté pan** over medium heat begin sautéing the onion in the oil. After about a minute add the mushrooms. After another minute add the garlic. After 1–2 minutes more remove from burner and set aside.

* In a **medium saucepan** over low heat, combine cream cheese, sour cream or yogurt, mozzarella, and Parmesan. When it begins to be smooth add the onion mixture, artichokes, spinach, and pepper. Cook this for about 2–3 minutes (until the fresh spinach is cooked). It can be enjoyed at this point OR you could put it into an **oven dish** with the Fontina cheese on top. (To save money, use mozzarella cheese for this instead.) Let it melt and slightly brown under the broiler for a more elegant (and delicious) presentation.

# Dressings, Sauces, and Seasoning Mixes

## Traditional French Vinaigrette
(Elimination-diet friendly)

A French chef in Alsace showed me these vinaigrettes many years ago.
Use a jar of any size. This is in "parts" by eye rather than measured amounts.

One third good vinegar (I like white balsamic but apple cider vinegar may be used)
One third EVOO
One third avocado oil or grapeseed oil

That's it. He said that it should never be shaken but stirred and spooned onto the salad. Just reporting what the Frenchman said. I do shake it sometimes…but he is right about the delicate touch.

## Mustard Vinaigrette
(Elimination-diet friendly)

Same as above but the vinegar part is half Dijon mustard and half vinegar.

## Sherry Vinaigrette

Same as "Traditional Vinaigrette" but the vinegar part is half sherry and half vinegar.

## Sesame Dressing
(Contains soy and sesame)

2 T. rice wine vinegar
1 T. tamari
1 T. sesame oil

## Tamari Ginger Sauce
(Contains soy)

If you enjoy Asian flavors, this is wonderful to use in many ways in your cooking, or at the table as a dipping sauce or the enhancement of rice, vegetables—basically anything! The idea of mixing the vinegar and tamari comes straight from China as they use vinegar and soy sauce for dipping dumplings. I happen to love ginger and cannot get enough of it and the green onions are ubiquitous in good Asian-style flavor. Hen hao!

½ c. tamari sauce
¼ c. rice wine vinegar
1–2 T. fresh ginger, finely minced
1–2 T. green onion, finely minced

I use an **8 or 12 oz. jam jar**, and I don't even measure these things. This recipe is just to get you started and then later you can adjust your ingredients as you please.

Instead of pouring (which makes a big mess anyway) always spoon it out so that you can get a nice mix of all the ingredients.

## Mediterranean Dipping Sauce

1 c. plain full-fat yogurt (or DF sour cream, softened with a small amount of water)
½ t. granulated garlic
½ t. dried dill
½ t. white wine vinegar
Salt and pepper to taste

## Spicy Thai Peanut Salad Dressing

1 c. mild picante sauce
½ c. tomato juice
1–2 t. Thai pepper sauce
¼ c. peanut butter
½ t. fish sauce (the one with the squid on it is the best one)
2 T. peanut oil
2 t. lemon juice

## Barbecue Sauce

This makes plenty for a whole rack of ribs with extra for dipping—about 2 quarts.

Ingredients:
½ c. DF butter (1 stick)
1 whole lemon
1¾ c. onion, minced

4–5 cloves of garlic, pressed
28 oz. ketchup
1⅓ c. tomato juice
11 oz. vegetable juice (V-8)
1 ½ c. brown sugar (to measure brown sugar always pack it into the measuring cup)
¼ c. molasses
½ c. Worcestershire sauce
¼ c. white wine or apple cider vinegar
1 t. fresh ground black pepper
½ t. sea salt
2 t. liquid smoke flavoring

✳ Deseed and chop the entire lemon (yes, the peel too) until it is finely minced.
✳ In a **large saucepan** melt the butter on medium heat and add the lemon, onion, and garlic.
✳ When the onion is softened (not brown) add the rest of the ingredients. Bring it to boiling and then turn the heat down to a simmer.
✳ Simmer, stirring every 5–10 minutes until it thickens. This will take about an hour to an hour and a half.

### Fruited Balsamic Vinegar

I started making this when we had just run out of some very fancy safe fruited balsamic vinegar. Everyone loves this.

Ingredients:
1–3 bottles of safe balsamic vinegar (Modena)
2–3 lbs. various fruits and it is fine if they have gotten overripe or even a little dried out.
I have used peaches, pears, apples and oranges in any combination.

✳ Pour all the vinegar into a **large heavy pot** on the stove. Set bottles aside.
✳ Wash and cut all fruit just in half or quarters and add to vinegar.
✳ Heat on medium-low. Let it mull for a couple of hours. Sorry about the strong aroma, but they'll get used to it about once a year because it tastes so great!
✳ Through a **strainer** and a **funnel** pour it slowly back into the bottles.
✳ Make a pretty label with the date. No refrigeration is needed.

For the seasonings that follow, I always use a **mortar and pestle**. It is the best way to crush everything to a consistent fine grain. Sea salt is usually a bit coarse anyway but this helps to crush things like seeds and rosemary. If you do not have a mortar and pestle you can still mix together prepared dried and ground spices and herbs. You will want to put the extra into a **small container or spice jar**.

### Hamburger Seasoning

¾ t. salt
1 t. granulated garlic
1½ t. dried oregano
½ t. fresh ground black pepper

I like to add a pinch of this to the kids' individual containers of "Fruited Balsamic Vinegar" and olive oil for their lunch salads.

### Lamb Seasoning

1 t. salt
1 ½ t. granulated garlic
1 ½ t. dried rosemary
1 t. dried oregano

### Creole Seasoning

1 t. salt
1 t. sugar
1 t. sweet paprika
½ t. lemon-pepper seasoning (make sure it does not contain MSG)
½ t. granulated garlic
¼ t. cayenne

# Main Courses

## Meats and Poultry

HACCP (Hazard Analysis & Critical Control Point) minimum temperatures:
Poultry, stuffed meats: 165° (73° C)
ground beef, veal, lamb, or pork: 160° (71° C)
beef, pork, veal, lamb steaks, roasts, or chops: 145° (63° C)

Test the thickest part of the meat with a meat thermometer (don't go all the way through to the pan).

*Roast Pork Shoulder—Someone could not resist tearing off a little of that crust right out of the oven!*

## Roast Pork Butt or Shoulder (Fresh Ham)
(Elimination-diet friendly)

My mother showed me this very simple way to roast this large cut of pork. If you don't see one in the grocery store without rind (skin) you can ask the butcher to cut it off for you. But tell him to leave a good layer of fat—it protects the meat while it roasts. If there is no one to do this you can do it yourself but it is not easy. It takes some muscle, a sharp knife, and good control. It will probably add another twenty minutes to your prep time to carefully cut the thick skin and not too much fat. Unless you know some people with pastured pigs and can get it from them, you will probably never find one that is organic, however, I recommend that you try this anyway because it is tender and delicious!

Ingredients:
9–10 lb. bone-in pork butt, rind removed
4 c. organic chicken broth or water

* Set the oven to bake at 350°.
* Place the pork fat side up in a **wide roasting pan** (which can just be the bottom part of your broiling pan) and pour the chicken broth into the pan around the meat.
* Roast (bake) the pork about 25 minutes per pound. If it is really big you may have to add some water to the pan halfway through the cooking.
* You could sprinkle a little salt and pepper on top but it amazingly needs nothing.
* Doneness should always be checked with a thermometer (at least 145 degrees).

It is very easy to make some gravy because you will have a lot of good meat juice but you will want to skim off the fat. This is more difficult not being able to cool it. **Strain** the juices into a **glass bowl** and after a moment you will see what is fat and what is not. Use a **shallow spoon** to skim the fat and discard it in the trash (unless you have a pastured pork butt, in which case this lard is good for cooking and you could put it in a separate container for the refrigerator or freezer).

## Steak
(Elimination-diet friendly)

Sirloin, ribeye, flank—the one I can always count on finding grass-fed and is the most tender (except for the tenderloin or filet mignon) is the ribeye.

They taste great broiled plain but you can add some salt and pepper or maybe the "Hamburger Seasoning" if you want—most rubs, however, will *not* be e-diet friendly.

Put the top rack on the highest level inside the oven and turn it on to broil. Always broil with the oven door ajar. There should be a spot where the door stays open with 4 to 6 inches of space.

Lay them on the top part of the **broiler pan**. There is a top with long narrow holes and indentations to fit on the pan bottom (which catches the juice and grease) so that air flows around while the meat is broiling.

Broil 4–5 minutes on each side or until done the way you like.
Broiling Note: It is important to watch carefully as you broil any type of meat, much like outdoor grilling, as the thickness of steaks and chops vary.

## Pork Chops
(Elimination-diet friendly)

Cook them the same way as the steaks but if they are really thick you may need to put the oven rack on one level lower than the highest. Turn them two or three more times to cook them evenly.

*When you are no longer on the elimination diet*, you could marinate the chops ahead for at least half an hour (or even the day before) using:

3 T. EVOO
½ c. tamari
2 T. cornstarch
2 T. Chinese cooking wine (optional)

Mix these ingredients inside a strong plastic bag or a **casserole dish** and then arrange the pork chops so that they are covered. Refrigerate. You do not need to have them submerged, but simply turn them over halfway through marinating time.

## Lamb Chops
(Elimination-diet friendly)

Cook these the same way as the steaks but start with only 3 minutes per side. You really do not want to overcook lamb. You could sprinkle "Lamb Seasoning" on them before you cook them. See "Lamb Pops" recipe for discussion of temperatures.

## Lamb Pops
(Elimination diet friendly)

These are incredibly elegant tiny lamb chops, which are bought and cooked together as a "rack." They come in an uncut line of chops with the tiny rib bones protruding with the meat and fat stripped off which is called "Frenched." This is done so that when they get to the plate one can just pick them up by the bone. Thus, some people serve them as finger food at very elegant parties.

Ingredients:
1 or 2 8–10 inch racks of lamb chops
2 T. beef tallow (or butter or coconut oil if you have not made any)
1–2 T. "Lamb Seasoning"
"Mediterranean Dipping Sauce" (optional)
*Preheat oven to 350º.

✳ In a **large heavy pot**, melt the beef tallow (fat). When the pot is hot enough for a drop of water to sizzle and disappear brown all the available meat surfaces of each rack. You will have to hold it up carefully with **tongs** to get the ends done. It might take a minute or more for each part to brown. Be careful not to move it too much and use a **metal spatula** to carefully unstick each side when it is browned. You are trying not to rip off the sealed browned surfaces as you move it around.
✳ Remove the meat to your roasting pan.
✳ Sprinkle all sides with "Lamb Seasoning."
✳ Cover the Frenched bones with foil and roast 20–30 minutes.
✳ Use a meat thermometer to test for doneness. Traditionally it should read:

Rare: 115 to 120°F.
Medium-rare: 120 to 125°F.
Medium: 130 to 135°F.

Medium-well: 140 to 145°F.
Well-done: 150 to 155°F.

However, the USDA now does not condone anything below 145. The above temperatures are taking into account the fact that the temperature will continue to rise a few degrees after removal from the oven during resting period of 10–20 minutes.

Many people prefer lamb to be medium-rare.

* After the rack has rested, carefully cut between each of the ribs.
* Serve immediately. They are excellent either with or without "Mediterranean Dipping Sauce." (Do not use the sauce if on the elimination diet).

## Leg of Lamb
(Elimination-diet friendly)

Lamb is enhanced by any herbs. And do not forget garlic! You can choose a boneless one or one with the bone. If I get a boneless one I actually take off the stretchy net with which they keep it together because the beautiful crispy and flavorful edges tend to come off with it after cooking. However, I then need to tie it back up with string to keep it together so I do not suggest you do this the first time. A leg of lamb with the bone does not pose this issue.

* The day before or even just a couple of hours before you will roast your leg or lamb, in a **food processor** or a **mortar and pestle** puree or crush into a paste:
    6–8 cloves of garlic
    2 t. dried rosemary (maybe a little thyme, oregano, or even sage…lemon zest may be added)
    1 t. fresh ground pepper
    ½ t. salt (I use more)
* You can cut some small slits in the top of the meat or not. Either way, slather the paste all over the roast. It is best to do this ahead, refrigerate, and then take it out of the refrigerator an hour before you will begin cooking it.
* Preheat oven to 400°.
* Heat a **large heavy pot** and using the tips in Lamb Pops recipe brown all sides in:
    2 T. beef tallow (fat)
* Remove it to your **wide roasting pan.**

✳ Deglaze the pot with ½ a cup of water and add:
  ½ c. chicken or beef broth

✳ After cooking the broth together with the scrapings and fat in the pot, pour it into the roasting pan. At this point you might add:
  10–12 peeled medium-small potatoes
  (½ lb. whole white or Crimini mushrooms and/or large pieces of carrots)
  BUT carrots only if for elimination dieters.

✳ Cook it 20 minutes and then turn the heat down to 325° and then cook it 20 minutes per pound or until the meat thermometer says 125–135°.

✳ Remove the roast to your **server** and cover loosely with foil. The roast should rest before cutting at least ten and up to 30 minutes, time to do the following.

✳ Remove the potatoes (and other vegetables) to a warm **serving dish** and cover and keep warm.

✳ Deglaze the roasting pan on the stovetop using:
  ½ c. water or red wine

✳ Hold the pan with a **potholder** as you move the liquid around on top of the burner on medium, using a **spatula** to scrap up anything stuck on the pan.

✳ Pour this into a **saucepan**. Add:
  more chicken or beef broth to make it about two cups

✳ Cook the liquid for a couple of minutes, then **strain** it and transfer it back to the saucepan.

✳ In a mug, mix:
  ½ c. hot water
  2–3 T. cornstarch

✳ Add this to the saucepan and bring to a boil stirring until it thickens.

✳ Add salt to taste if necessary and serve this gravy with your sliced leg of lamb.

*Crispy Roast Chicken with roasted potatoes and celery root, sautéed Shanghai cabbage, and Israeli Salad.*

## Crispy Roasted Whole Chicken
(Elimination diet friendly)

Preheat oven to 350°.

Ingredients:
1 whole organic chicken (around 4.5 lbs. is a good size, and if you want to roast two of them
    it is about the same amount of time. Use the **thermometer**).
coconut oil cooking spray
sea salt
garlic powder
Balti spice (Do *not* include this for elimination diet, but you can use black pepper.)

This is a Pakistani-inspired mix I order from an excellent spice company that gives a lovely
warm flavor, but if you prefer, substitute with fresh ground black pepper.

I like to begin the operation at the sink because of the nature of poultry juices. I end up
thoroughly washing my hands a few times in the process.

* Set the packaged chicken in the sink.
* Have your **roasting pan**—the bottom half of a broiling pan does nicely—right beside
  the sink.
* Cut open the plastic at the cavity end just enough to reach in to remove the parts left
  inside by the packaging company.
* I like to roast the neck, giblets and heart next to the bird for use in the future together
  with the bones to make broth. Some people enjoy chicken livers and would know what
  to do with them but I throw them away. I am aware that this is a waste because organ
  meats are very good for us but I have not had the bravery yet to try to make anything
  with them.
* Pull the chicken out, letting the juice drain out, and place in roasting pan.
* Cleanly throw away the packaging with juices and wash and dry hands thoroughly.
* Spray coconut oil on the entire visible skin lightly all over moving the wings outward to
  cover the skin between them and the body.
* Wash and dry hands if you touched the chicken.
* Sprinkle liberally with sea salt and garlic powder and go with a little lighter but complete
  coverage with the Balti or pepper.

✳ Roast in the oven for about 1½ hours until the skin is beautifully browned and the juices are no longer pinkish. To test this insert a **large meat fork** into the cavity so that the bird can be tipped up to see the color of the juice that runs out. If you do not feel good about this method insert a **thermometer** into a thick area of the meat to see the proper HAACP temperature to be 165°.

✳ Your roast chicken should be crispy golden brown on the outside and tender and juicy on the inside. Let it rest for 10 minutes. The joints should be relatively easy to separate with a knife.

✳ Scrape and pour the drippings into a container, cover and refrigerate until you are ready to add it to the bones to make broth.

## Roast Duck
(Elimination-diet friendly)

Ingredients:
1 whole duck
grapeseed or coconut oil spray
2 star anise or 1½ t. ground star anise
1 ¼ t. salt
4 black pepper corns or ½ t. fresh ground pepper
¼ t. granulated garlic
1 t. onion powder

✳ Preheat oven to 350°.

✳ Mix or crush together in a **mortar and pestle** the star anise, salt, pepper, garlic, and onion.

✳ Similar to "Crispy Roasted Whole Chicken," remove the duck from packaging and place it in your roasting pan. Remove any paper or plastic from the giblets and let them cook inside or alongside the duck.

✳ Spray with oil and then sprinkle liberally with spice mix the entire skin of the duck.

✳ Roast about 1 ½ hr. or until internal temperature is 165°.

Note: If the skin is not browned you might want to run it under the broiler for a couple of minutes. Be there to make sure that it does not scorch the top.

✳ To serve, it is best if the duck is cut so that there is skin and fat on every piece to be eaten with each piece of meat.

✳ Now you have some excellent duck fat with which to cook other things. Just heat, strain and pour the drippings into a heat safe jar. The fat will rise up to the surface as it cools. Refrigerate. If you remove the hardened fat to a different container you can use the delicious concentrated juices to flavor vegetables or rice.

*Steak Chili with my own homemade gluten-free, dairy-free, rice-free bread (the recipe for which I will give another time).*

## Steak Chili
(Contains beans)

There are, of course, easier ways to make chili but the variety of high-quality ingredients in this recipe make it a magnificent meal.

✳ Prepare the steak as per "Steak" under "Meats and Poultry."

As I mentioned in my "Approach to Food" section, I usually buy an extra steak to broil along with the four I broil for us when we have them for dinner. It is much easier to trim fat and gristle after it has been cooked. After our steak dinner I usually have a couple of half steaks left and this extra one.

✳ Trim and cut the steak.

I trim whatever is left and I might set aside about ½–¾ c. of trimmed and cut steak for Ethan's lunch the next day. The rest I cut very small so that it is easy to chew in the chili and then I put it in the fridge until I am ready to use it in the chili.

✳ I immediately put all the fat and gristly parts into a **saucepan** with water covering it and start it to simmer for liquid I will be adding to the chili.
✳ Wash, peel, trim, and cut into small dice:
    2 large carrots
    2–4 stalks of celery (depending on their size)
✳ Set aside.
✳ Prepare and chop:
    1–2 onions, small dice
✳ Into a **large stew/stock pot** put:
    2 T. beef tallow or chicken fat (or DF butter)
✳ Over med-high heat, add the onion, lightly season with salt, and sauté for 3–5 minutes.
✳ Add carrots and celery and sauté for 10–12 minutes over low heat. Do not let them dry out—you might have to add a little liquid from the saucepan—but not too much.
✳ While they cook cut your peppers.
    2–3 red, green, and/or orange bell peppers or some hotter ones such as poblano and serrano…or even no peppers…chili can be any way you want it…add the peppers.
✳ Add the beef to the veggies and sprinkle with:
    2 T. regular chili powder
✳ Combine everything and sauté adding a little more sea salt.

✳ After the beef is uniform in color add some liquid from the pan of beef trimmings. You might want to put all of it in and then add more water to the trimmings to make more beef liquid.

✳ Add:
  2 15-oz. cans of pink, red, or black beans
  28-oz. can of diced tomatoes

✳ When it all comes to a boil (bubbling) turn the heat down to low. Cook this all together for at least another 30 minutes, stirring about every five minutes to keep it from sticking to the bottom. Add more liquid during this time. By the end, it should be thickened, the vegetables cooked, and the flavors well married.

✳ Add salt if desired or let individuals season their own bowl of chili.

## Hamburger Stew

I know that the name of this may not excite but I have kept it because it is almost exactly what our babysitter made sometimes when we were staying over. It was my favorite dinner and may be the first thing I was ever interested in trying to make (other than cookies and cakes). Chasey (Mrs. Chase) always served it over white rice and called it "Hamburger Stew on Rice." These days I hardly ever eat it with rice because I like it so much by itself and it makes the greatest Sloppy Joe, which my son loves. More importantly, large amounts of it can be made so that the "extra" can be refrigerated or frozen to be used later as the meat portion of Shepherd's Pie or Lasagna. It is basically Chasey's to which I added onion and apple.

Ingredients:
1 T. chicken or beef fat (see my section on bone broth and rendered fat). If you don't have any yet use your cooking oil of choice (coconut, avocado, or EVOO)
2 c. onion, small dice
1 apple, peeled, cored, and small diced (optional, but I really recommend it!)
2 lb. grass-fed ground beef
28 oz. tomato sauce (but use less if it is very thick)
½ t. garlic powder
½ t. salt
½ t. fresh ground pepper

✳ In a **large frying pan or skillet** melt the fat and when the temp is up (it will sizzle lightly with a drop of water) add the onion. Sauté for 5 minutes.

✳ Add apple and sauté 2–3 minutes.

✳ Add the beef carefully breaking it up to a consistent texture stirring until the meat is consistently browned. If at this point, there is an excessive amount of fat, pour it off into a Pyrex bowl or into the trash. I always save such a thing because it is good fat with which to cook at a later time and usually comes with some very good meat juice, which is useful for flavoring vegetables or soup…

✳ Add the remaining ingredients and simmer for 10–15 minutes until the liquid has been reduced.

This is really great kid food and can be put into a thermos for a hot lunch… You can add a small container of grated fresh parmesan or some DF parmesan and some crackers…

## Lambites or Lamburgers

Ingredients:
1 medium onion, minced
2 T. DF butter
6 cloves of garlic, pressed
¼ c. sherry
2 lbs. ground lamb
2 T. parsley, minced
1 T. Worcestershire sauce
1 T. dried dill
¼ t. fresh ground nutmeg
1 T. lemon zest
½ t. salt
½ t. fresh ground pepper
coconut oil or avocado oil for cooking

✳ In a **small frying pan** sauté the onion in the butter until glossy, add the garlic and then the sherry.
✳ When the onion is just starting to brown turn off the burner (the liquid should be gone).
✳ Let it cool a bit and then in a **medium bowl** mix the onions with the parsley first so that it wilts and then add the rest of the ingredients. Hand mix them together well.
✳ Form 1–2 T. patties for Lambites (should make 40–45).
✳ Or form larger patties into burgers.
✳ Fry them in a little coconut or avocado oil (or a mixture of the two). Do not overcook!

Delicious by themselves or perhaps dipped in "Mediterranean Dipping Sauce."

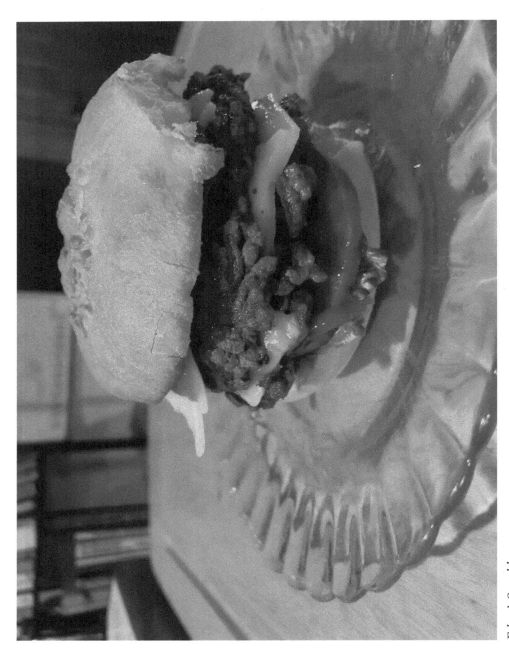

*Ethan's Smashburger*

## Smashburgers
(Elimination-diet friendly)

Ethan made me get him a **cast iron skillet** and a very fine and proper **narrow but heavy-duty metal spatula** so he could make these! But Nina said, "officially my favorite homemade hamburger I've ever had!" So it was worth it!

1–2 lbs. grass-fed ground beef
3–6 T. beef tallow or other fat
"Hamburger Seasoning"

✳ Make medium large-sized meatballs (1.5–2 oz. ea.)
✳ Have the skillet very hot. Melt 2 T. fat to start with.
✳ Make 4 at a time quickly smashing them down as soon as they hit the surface.
✳ Sprinkle each with "Hamburger Seasoning."
✳ When they are well-browned, turn and mash them again.
✳ Ethan says they should be crispy around the edges.
✳ Remove to paper towel lined plate.
✳ Scrape the pan, removing any large particles and adding 1 T. more fat.
✳ Repeat until all are done.

## Italian Turkey Meatballs
(Gluten—and grain-free, dairy-free)

*Or **beef** can be used to make them more traditional*
Contains soy and egg

We all love these and Ethan always eats a lot of them the day I make them. I found that it is a great help to have **1 or 2 mini muffin pans** in which to help the meatballs keep their form in the beginning of the cooking. I freeze containers of ten in their sauce for easy thawing and the choice for their use later, saving some for the fridge for lunch or dinner the next day.

Ingredients:
2 lbs. ground turkey, preferably organic (or grass-fed ground beef)
1 c. uncooked quick-cooking gluten-free oats
2 T. EVOO plus more for the muffin tin(s)
1 medium-large onion minced

¼ c. sherry (optional)
½ c. minced fresh parsley
1–2 T. minced fresh basil or 1 T. dried basil
2 cloves garlic minced or pressed
2 eggs
1½ T. Worcestershire sauce
½ t. paprika
½ t. fresh ground pepper
1 t. salt
6 cups marinara sauce (or half marinara half tomato sauce)

Note: To save a little time, I mince the onion first and then work on mincing all that parsley while the onion is cooking. You could use a food processor, but I think that the amounts don't warrant it because of the time it takes to clean the thing. Your choice.

* Preheat oven to 350 degrees.
* In a **small frying pan** sauté the onion in olive oil at a low temperature. After about 2–3 minutes add the sherry. Sauté until tender and the liquid is absorbed/reduced. Set aside.
* In a **large bowl,** add the eggs, scrambling them with a **fork** and then incorporate with a drop or two of EVOO.
* Add parsley, basil, garlic, Worcestershire sauce, sautéed onion, paprika, pepper, and salt and incorporate.
* Add turkey and incorporate everything well.
* Drip a little EVOO into each cup of a **mini muffin pan**. Use the fork to scoop a medium-small meatball-sized clump of your mix into each cup. *Be careful not to push down or overfill them.* If you are using beef you do not need the muffin tin but instead form balls and just use your **9" x 13" pan**. Turkey is harder to do than traditional meatballs because the mix is so loose. Also, unless you have a second mini muffin pan it is important that you *refrigerate the raw turkey mix* each time you finish filling the pan to bake them.
* Bake meatballs 11–12 minutes to set. Let cool briefly. While the turkey meatballs are in the oven, pour marinara-tomato sauce into a **9"×13" oven dish**. Gently remove baked meatballs placing them carefully in the sauce. It is important that you are gentle—and DO NOT EAT any of them YET—because they are not fully cooked. For meatballs made with beef everything is easier because they hold together better. Just pour in the marinara-tomato sauce and go to the next step.
* When all the meatballs have been baked for the first time and are now in the sauce, gently move them around to settle evenly and to have a covering of the sauce over them.

They will not actually be submerged and some will be almost half-way above the level of the sauce.

❋ Bake them in the oven dish 45 minutes.

Enjoy with pasta, or make a meatball sub (a "grinder" where I came from) on a gluten-free roll toasted with (or without) dairy or non-dairy mozzarella cheese.

Afterthought: Having gone the mini muffin tin route a few times, I realized that I had an unused **cake-pop maker** in the basement that had been a gift some time ago. What a mess it made! But the meatballs obtained when I finally got good at using that cake-pop maker were perfectly shaped and partially crisped. We all agreed that it was a great improvement. However, it is so difficult to clean the grease and bits out of this little cake ball maker, I think it will not be worth it to the busy cook.

## Lasagna
(Dairy-free, egg free, contains lentil)

To satisfy everyone in our house I used to make two lasagnas so that one was dairy-free. I struggled to use the brown rice noodles (even though they weren't good for me or Ethan). They were such a pain because they had to be precooked like gluten pasta and then somehow handled in this state without breaking. Didn't make it very often. I finally saw these fabulous noodles made from lentils. There is still some brown rice in this product but much reduced because lentil takes up 50 percent of its mass. However, the outstanding attribute is that these noodles are ready to use with no precooking! Also, I, one of the last people still eating dairy around here, like the dairy-free "ricotta" part of my American lasagna better than actual ricotta.

This recipe will work for a single **9"×13" oven dish**.

Lasagna is very adaptable to different tastes. I have written this recipe out to give the reader an example with measurements to start with and fully encourage the cook to make adjustments according to the family's tastes.

Because of the way that lasagna is "built" I have listed the ingredients for each type of layer followed by each of their instructions followed then by lasagna layer construction and baking.

Beef Layer (or turkey instead):
1 T. chicken or beef fat
2 c. onion, small dice
2 lb. grass-fed ground beef (or organic turkey)
28 oz. tomato sauce
½ t. garlic powder
½ t. salt
½ t. fresh ground pepper

✳ In a **large frying pan** melt the fat and when the temp is up (it will sizzle lightly with a drop of water) add the onion. Sauté for 5 minutes.
✳ Add the beef or turkey carefully breaking it up to a consistent texture stirring until the meat is consistently browned. If at this point, there is an excessive amount of fat, pour it off into a Pyrex bowl or into the trash. I always save such a thing because it is good fat with which to cook at a later time and usually comes with some very good meat juice, which is useful for flavoring vegetables or soup…
✳ Add the remaining ingredients and simmer for 10–15 minutes.
✳ Set aside.

You will notice that this is my Hamburger Stew/Sloppy Joe recipe.
I encourage the maker to make a lot so that some of it goes into the freezer.

✳ If you have it already, use:
    4 c. thawed "Hamburger Stew"

Sauce:
Ingredients:
1–2 qt. well-seasoned marinara sauce
½ c. water
OR MAKE it yourself with:
28 oz. whole peeled tomatoes
28 oz. plain tomato sauce
1–2 t. dried basil
½–1 t. dried oregano
1 t. garlic powder (or you can press 1 or 2 cloves fresh garlic)
½ t. sea salt
½ t. fresh ground pepper

✳ Into a **medium-large saucepan** squeeze each of the whole tomatoes through your fingers, crushing or removing the stem center as you go along. While you are at it, you can also remove any skin the tomato company has left on them. The end product is not overly smooth but not lumpy (as in, if I had used diced tomatoes).

✳ Add the rest of the ingredients, bring to a boil, turn the burner down and simmer for a few minutes and then remove from heat. Normally, when I make pasta sauce I would simmer much longer, but here it is important to retain as much liquid as possible so that the lentil noodles can soak it up during the lasagna baking.

Vegetable Layer:
Frozen Roasted Green Tomatoes
I recommend that you try the green tomato recipe for your veggie layer because of the nice tang it gives the lasagna. However, it may be too difficult for you to find the ingredients for it…

zucchini, cut into ⅜"–½" disks OR
eggplant, peeled and sliced ⅜" thickness
EVOO, sea salt and fresh ground pepper (for drizzling and seasoning if you are using zucchini or eggplant)
You could also skip this layer, but why would you pass up any opportunity to tuck vegetables into your family's diet?

"Cheese" Layer:
2½ c. DF sour cream
1 t. dried basil
salt and pepper to taste
In a **medium-sized bowl** mix these ingredients together well.

Noodle:
2 packages lentil lasagna
Divide the 2 boxes into three equal piles.

sliced pepperoni (optional)
Ordinarily, lasagna is topped with mozzarella, which protects. I cover the top with pepperoni for this purpose and usually remove it afterward because they have gotten burnt. If you do not like the idea of pepperoni you could just cover the whole thing with foil halfway through cooking.

Now that you have each of the lasagna layers assembled, you are ready to lay them in your **9"×13" baking dish.**

Preheat oven to 375°.
Layers from bottom to top:

| | |
|---|---|
| 1st layer | thick coating of marinara sauce |
| 2nd layer | several sheets of lasagna |
| 3rd layer | Roasted Green Tomatoes |
| | (or zucchini or eggplant drizzled and seasoned) |
| 4th layer | several sheets of lasagna |
| 5th layer | ground beef or turkey mixture |
| 6th layer | several sheets of lasagna |
| 7th layer | "cheese" mixture |
| 8th layer | thick coating of marinara sauce |
| 9th layer | pepperoni (optional) |

Bake it for about one hour. It may take a bit longer than the package says, so check, and if the noodle is not cooked you should keep baking it, now at a lower temperature. I turned it down to about 340 and settled on baking it another hour to ensure that the noodle is fully cooked.

I made one half the size of the one here and worried so, that it would dry up, that I covered the whole thing, from the beginning, with aluminum foil. Very moist but undercooked at the hour mark. I loosened the cover and put it back in with it able to vent.

## Mediterranean Spaghetti Squash
### (Optional dairy)

2–3 lb. spaghetti squash
2 T. olive oil
28 oz. diced tomatoes
4–6 cloves of garlic
¼ c. fresh basil, minced, or 1 T. dried basil
1½ t. fresh oregano, minced, or 1 t. dried oregano
½ c. green olives, chopped coarsely
½ c. golden raisins
4 oz. feta cheese (optional)

✳  Wash spaghetti squash and cut it in half lengthwise removing strings and seeds.

If cutting a spaghetti squash (or any other large squash, some of which are exceedingly hard-shelled) is a daunting prospect, ask the produce team at your grocery store to cut it in half for you. They can also wrap the cut pieces in plastic.

✳  Brush each half with olive oil and sprinkle with salt and pepper, place cut side up on an **edged baking sheet** and bake at 375° for about 45–60 minutes. **Or** you can also microwave in a **covered dish** on high power for 10 to 12 minutes but you will probably have to do each side separately. Either way, because each squash is different it may take a little more or less time. Test to see if a fork will free the strings of the squash easily but do not let it get mushy.
✳  Heat the olive oil in a **saucepan** over medium heat and with a **garlic press** add the garlic to the pan.
✳  Cook about 1 minute and then add the tomatoes. When they come to a gentle boil add the basil and oregano. Let this simmer for a few minutes.
✳  When the squash is done, carefully using a **fork**, scrape the squash pulp into a **warm serving dish** so that it comes in strands.
✳  Add the tomatoes, olives, and raisins, gently combining so that the ingredients are still visible atop the squash. Grind fresh black pepper over the dish.
✳  Serve it with feta cheese on the side or not at all if you have dairy intolerance.

## Shepherd's Pie
(Gluten-free, dairy-free, corn can be optional)

This makes a lot of shepherd's pie. It is a lot of work to make this so I like to freeze some smaller ones. You can make it in one **9"×13" oven dish** plus another **5–7" diameter oven dish** for the freezer. You could also make **two medium ones** plus a **couple of smaller ones**. It depends on the dishes with which you have to work. You might even decide to make a few single serving sized pies in **ramekins**—great to take to work and just microwave when you want to eat. I occasionally take one to my grandparents for their dinner—they love it! It is up to you. As I said, it does take some time so you might as well get some mileage out of it.

15 medium potatoes
1 c. chicken stock/broth
2 T. avocado or olive oil or, if you prefer, DF butter
salt
fresh ground pepper

1 T. beef fat
1 medium-large onion, small dice
2½–3 lb. ground organic beef
½ t. sea salt
15 oz. tomato sauce

2 c. carrots, small dice (about 8 carrots)
1 c. celery, small dice
16 oz. green beans, trimmed and cut into segments (or 15 oz. can)
15 oz. sweet corn (optional)
1½ c. frozen peas

sea salt and fresh black pepper
coconut oil spray

✳ Wash, peel, cut in halves or quarters, and boil potatoes in a **heavy pot** until soft but not falling apart (10–15 minutes) drain and place back in the heavy pot.

✳ Mash the potatoes and add chicken stock and oil. Optional: you may add instead of the oil 2 T dairy-free butter. Salt and fresh ground pepper to taste—really whip them so that they are smooth. Set aside.

✳ In a **large frying pan**, sauté onion in the fat for 2–3 minutes. Add sea salt and ground beef using a **spatula** to separate and move the beef around until it is a uniform crumble and brown color. Add tomato sauce and simmer until reduced, about 15–25 minutes. *Turn off and set aside.

✳ Preheat oven to 350°.

✳ In a **large bowl** combine carrots, celery, green beans, corn and peas. You can instead use 6 cups of frozen mixed vegetables to save time but it will not contain celery unless you add it to 5 c. of the frozen veggies. Add about ¼ t. each of sea salt and fresh ground pepper and microwave it covered for 3-4 minutes.

✳ Now you are ready to assemble your beautiful shepherd's pies. Put about two inches of vegetable mix on the bottom of each baking dish. Gently pack it in so that it won't move around easily.

✳ Spread one to two inches of meat mixture next, and then at least two inches of mashed potato to cover the top. Try to make them level with the top of the dishes you are going to freeze. You can mound up the potato a little bit on the one you are eating right away.

✳ Always put a pan under them as they cook because the juices can overflow.

✳ Spray the tops with a little coconut oil.

✳ Bake for about an hour or until you see the juices bubbling around the edge of the potato.

To freeze:

✳ Cut **parchment paper** to fit perfectly on top of the potato.

✳ Place in a strong plastic bag and seal with twist tie or zip. It is important to remove all the air possible. You can do this by closing the bag to a small opening through which the air is sucked out either directly with the mouth or using an inserted straw.

✳ Medium-sized frozen shepherd's pie should be baked for an hour. It is less for the little ones, but 5–10 min in the microwave may be a better way to go in this case. Because microwaves vary it is important to know that the safe temperature to which microwaved food should be warmed is 165 degrees.

### New England Crab Cakes
(Can be made elimination-diet friendly; contains crab and shrimp)

One day in October 2014 I just happened to be watching as a chef on TV was about to create crab cakes without breadcrumbs for binding. I was thrilled to discover the use of shrimp for this purpose because crab cakes are always off the menu for us anywhere crab cakes are made. Now we can make them and enjoy them at home.

These can be E-diet friendly by simply leaving out the Old Bay Seasoning and hot sauce. (Not quite as fun, I know, but still quite delicious—add some black pepper!)

My family loves these by themselves or with some ketchup and with or without a toasted GF roll. I believe that many people like tartar sauce (which, like ketchup and the roll, would not be E-diet acceptable) so the ingredient label must be checked for hidden gluten. Or one could make some tartar sauce by mixing acceptable store-bought mayonnaise and minced pickles.

Ingredients:
7 medium or 5–6 large raw shrimp
⅓ c. celery, chopped (about 1 stalk)
⅓ c. Italian parsley (3–6 sprigs)
⅓ c. scallions, chopped (2–3 green onions)
1½ t. Old Bay Seasoning

3 T. Dijon mustard

1 T. hot sauce (I like sriracha—anything will do as long as you have checked that there is no hidden gluten in the ingredients)

1 lb. can of Lump or Jumbo Lump Crabmeat

2–5 T. (maybe more) chicken fat or coconut oil for frying

✻ Prepare a **cookie sheet or tray** that will fit in your refrigerator with a piece of parchment paper.

✻ Puree in a **food processor** the shrimp, celery, parsley, scallions, Old Bay Seasoning, Dijon mustard, and hot sauce.

✻ In a **medium-sized bowl** gently go through the crabmeat using your fingers to remove any pieces of shell.

✻ Gently with a **soft spatula or your hands** incorporate the pureed ingredients with the crabmeat.

✻ With your hands, form about 9 medium-sized crab cakes or, for an appetizer, multiple mini bite-sized cakes or balls. Place each on the parchment. Place the tray in the refrigerator for at least 30 minutes.

✻ Now that they are set, they can be fried in a **frying pan** at a medium heat in chicken fat or coconut oil—just enough to cover the bottom of the pan about ¼–⅜ inch deep—not a deep fry. Let them cook for several minutes on each side without disturbing them too much. They should be nicely browned and firm.

✻ As each one is finished, remove to a **plate with paper towels**. Serve immediately, or they can be cooled and later quickly reheated in the microwave or a lightly greased frying pan.

We have also found that the **air fryer** is an amazing tool for cooking crab cakes because the only oil used is where the racks are sprayed or brushed with coconut oil or other convenient grease.

### Simple Salmon Bake
(Elimination-diet friendly)

This recipe is small because my family does not unanimously love salmon. It can be done with any amount of salmon. Cooking times vary, but this is also a good way to cook halibut, cod, haddock, and Chilean sea bass.

1 lb. wild caught salmon (hopefully a thick steak)

coconut oil spray

sea salt
fresh ground pepper

I love to bake right in our **toaster oven**. It takes no time to preheat and doesn't heat the whole kitchen. I believe it was our favorite wedding present and was still going 14 years later. Funny thing is that it stopped working not long after I wrote that! New one's not quite as great but I still bake or broil small things in it. Of course, this can also be done in a conventional oven.

* Preheat oven temperature to 325°.
* Spray the bottom of the pan with coconut oil—this can be a **cookie sheet with edges** or the **bottom of your broiling pan** or any **oven-safe dish**. (If you miss this step the skin sticks really well to the pan!)
* Lay the fish skin side down in the oven dish.
* Spray the fish lightly with coconut oil.
* Sprinkle sea salt and grind a bit of pepper over the salmon.
* Put them in the oven and check them at 12–15 minutes. *Do not overcook.* They may need a few more minutes to cook them depending on the thickness of the salmon steaks. It should be tender and easily come away from the skin on the bottom when serving.

### Beautiful Grouper (or Orange Roughy or Tilapia)
**elimination diet friendly**

Ingredients:
1 lb. fish
Adobo seasoning
Dijon mustard

* Preheat oven to 350°.
* Lay out the fish in an oven dish.
* Sprinkle with adobo seasoning.
* Splatter with some Dijon mustard.
* Bake 15–20 minutes.

Serving suggestion: With "Sautéed Baby Kale" and "Tomato and Cucumber Salad."

# Main Course Sauces

*"Cream" Sauce with Ham and Peas and Israeli Cabbage Salad.*

## "Cream" Sauce with Peas and Ham
### (Dairy-free, contains garbanzo bean)

My favorite Italian pasta was Pasta Carbonara, which contains prosciutto instead of ham, but this preparation comes close to the real thing and everyone in the family loves it.

If soy cannot be tolerated, I have found that the flavor is still quite good with all the dairy-free cheese and sour cream left out.

3 c. chicken broth
3–4 T. nondairy butter
½ c. nondairy mozzarella
½ c. nondairy sour cream
½ c. garbanzo bean flour
fresh ground black pepper
1 pkg. (9 oz.) frozen peas
¾ lb. uncured ham, small cubed or like thick matchsticks
¼ c. sherry (optional—makes it taste gourmet but the sauce is fine without it)

✳ In a **medium saucepan** bring chicken broth to a boil adding the butter, cheese, and sour cream. Use a **whisk** to stir until everything is melted and well incorporated. Keep whisking as you add the bean flour. Keep whisking as the flour cooks. This will take about 5–10 minutes. The hardest thing about this recipe is that one must stand there whisking until it thickens. Believe me, it is worth it.
✳ Add plenty of fresh ground black pepper.
✳ When the sauce is thickened, turn the burner down to low and add the peas, ham, and the sherry if you want it. Bring this back up to a low bubbling simmer for at least 10–15 minutes stirring occasionally. You may want to add more pepper.
✳ Serve over pasta or this can be a soup as is.

My Favorite Gluten-Free Pasta

My favorite pasta is a delicious brand of organic corn-quinoa rotini.

Other choices are brown rice pasta, corn pasta, and pasta made from lentils or soy. There are different blends of the various non-wheat flours from which these pastas are made many of which rice is an element. The shopper will find organic or GMO-free verified varieties and others that do not say and therefore have conventional (GMO) ingredients.

## DF Spinach-Artichoke Sauce
(Dairy-free, contains garbanzo bean)

Ingredients:
2 c. chicken stock/broth
½ c. garbanzo bean flour
1–2 c. chopped preserved artichoke hearts
5 oz. baby spinach
3 Crimini mushrooms, sliced thinly
1 T. avocado oil
⅛–¼ t. fresh ground pepper

* In a **small frying pan** heat the avocado oil and sauté the mushrooms until a little browned. Turn it off and set mushrooms aside.
* In a **saucepan** bring the chicken broth to a boil and **whisk** in the garbanzo bean flour. Keep whisking to prevent lumps until the sauce thickens.
* Add the chopped artichoke and the spinach and stir with a **spoon** or **spatula** instead. When the spinach is cooked down—it will be darker green—add the mushrooms and the pepper.

This can be used as a pasta sauce or even a base for a casserole…

I thought that it might be possible to make it with brown rice flour instead of chickpea flour if there was sensitivity or allergy to beans…but I have not tried to make it that way and so I do not know if it can be substituted with the same amount.

# Desserts

*Brownies or Chocolate in Fives.*

## Brownies or Chocolate in Fives
(Contains egg, dairy-free)

I know that there are many GF brownie mixes to be found, but I invite you to make this easy scratch recipe and you may never want to use any of those (unless you are out of your own kitchen wanting to whip up something sweet for your family to eat while others enjoy their glutenous sweets, in which case you need also to buy the aluminum pan the right size to bake them in).

**About the flour**: The thing about brownies is that there is so little wheat flour in a good brownie recipe that you can replace it with just about anything. Most people might opt for rice flour or a mixture of half rice and half tapioca flour, but I like to use Bob's Red Mill All-Purpose GF Flour because it has no rice in it. Sometimes I will use half BRM All-Purpose and half tapioca flour. Tapioca flour by itself can be used, however, I think that the result is too sticky, making cutting and transporting difficult. This is up to the cook to decide.

My Favorite Flour Mix For Brownies

½ c. BRM all-purpose GF flour
½ c. coconut flour
¼ c. cassava flour
2 t. arrowroot starch.

The point is that you can make it very simply using the types of easily accessible GF flours I list above or you can try some things with the more exotic flours which are not as prevalent in the grocery store. See Chapter 6 on shopping and planning.

**Important**: There are two things to be done in the beginning to carry out this recipe to perfection.

1) The eggs must be removed from the refrigerator well before so that they can be room temperature.
2) The chocolate and butter should be melted together *with enough time to cool down,* at least, to barely warm so that you do not cook the eggs prematurely when mixing these ingredients together.

Ingredients:
5 oz. unsweetened chocolate
½ c. dairy-free butter (1 stick)
5 medium-large eggs, room temperature
¼ t. salt
2½ c. sugar
1½ t. double strength vanilla extract
1¼ c. GF flour
coconut oil spray
DF chocolate morsels or chunks (optional)

✳ Preheat the oven to 325°.
✳ Spray a **9"×13" baking dish** with coconut oil.
✳ Melt and mix the chocolate and butter together. This can, of course, be done in the microwave but I prefer my **small double boiler** because I can do other things while it is heating without worry of burning the chocolate. Take it off the heat and set aside to cool. (Remove the top pan from the bottom so that the hot water does not keep your chocolate hot. Also, avoid getting any water in this mixture, as it will ruin it.) If you do not have a double boiler or a microwave oven, this can be done *carefully* in a **saucepan** over low heat being careful not to burn the chocolate—continuously stir and remove from heat before it comes to a boil.
✳ Into a **large bowl** break the eggs and **whisk** them until they are a little lighter in color and very frothy. Add the salt and begin to add the sugar about a ½ c. at a time actively whisking it to create more bubbles.
✳ After the sugar is dissolved (or close to it) add the vanilla.

With a **soft spatula** quickly fold in your cooled chocolate mixture and then the flour mixture trying to keep as much volume (bubbles) as possible.

✳ As soon as everything is blended together pour the batter in the baking dish.
✳ If you want chocolate morsels or chunks, bake the brownies for 12 minutes, remove the pan from the oven to sprinkle them evenly across the surface and return the brownies to the oven for 20–25 minutes more.
✳ Bake 35–40 minutes if not using extra chocolate morsels. Ovens vary, so always set the timer for a little less time and check them with a toothpick as you come close to end. The **toothpick (or wooden skewer)** should not withdraw any raw batter on it. I like them to be cooked through because they will still be moist, but if you prefer, you can bake a

couple minutes less. If they are too moist they will be hard to get out of the pan. Wait until they almost completely cool before cutting.

This recipe may at first seem involved but there is no comparing it to any box brownie, gluten-free or otherwise!

## Angel Food Cake
(Grain-free, dairy-free, contains egg)

The first time I made this it was devoured! This is a real old-school angel food cake.

I know the process may seem a little daunting and exacting as you read through this recipe, but I assure you that it is worth it. I would have listed the ingredients in the beginning but as you will see, the amounts of flour are measured out of larger amounts and you may possibly need more than 10 eggs at room temperature if one is not looking normal or you have broken an egg yolk…read on.

It is important to have a dozen eggs at room temperature before you start. This is vital. Since egg whites are the main ingredient and the real building blocks for the rising of the cake, it is beneficial to follow this recipe exactly. They should only be separated just before use and it is advisable to do each egg separately (in a small clear or white bowl) so that you can see that there is NO yolk. This also enables you to discard any discolored one before it goes into the rest of them.

It is also very important that there *not be any* grease residue on anything that the egg whites will touch in the process (i.e.: beaters, bowl, tube pan, etc.). If there is, or, if there is any yolk at all in the whites, they will not foam up when beaten and the cake will not be successful.

Angel food cake is baked in an **ungreased tube pan** that is made in two pieces. The tube helps to support the cake as it rises during baking. After it is done the whole thing is inverted immediately to cool and set for 1 ½ hours.

✳ For the flour in this cake, I put together:
 ⅔ c. tapioca flour
 ⅓ c. potato flour
 1 T. arrowroot

They must be sifted together 3 times before one cup is measured out for the cake. You could double or triple all of this so that the extra flour (closed carefully against moisture and labeled for angel cake) will be ready for the next time you want to make angel food. Always sift it again before measuring a cup out the next time because it would have settled and compressed.

✳ Preheat oven to 350°.

✳ You will need at least **three medium and small bowls** for the dry ingredients. Sift enough confectioner's sugar twice and then measure out:

  1¼ c. confectioner's sugar

 Out of this measurement take ¼ c. confectioner's sugar and sift it with:

  1 c. flour mixture (discussed above)

Note: Since it will probably fall right through the sifter, use a **fork or small whisk** to gently combine these dry ingredients.

✳ Separate into a **large mixing bowl** and start beating gently:

  10 egg whites (should be about 1½ c.)

  2 T. water

✳ When they are frothy add:

  1 t. cream of tarter

  1 t. vanilla extract

  ½ t. almond extract

  ½ t. salt

✳ Continue to beat the egg whites as you gradually increase the speed of the beaters to high, and begin to add the sugar little by little. (If you are beating by hand, the sugar should be added in the last half. Oh yes, I once made an angel food cake in college using two forks! A flat whip would have been ideal but I hardly knew anything about anything back then.) When the beating is finished, the egg/sugar mixture should hold lovely peaks without appearing dry.

✳ Very gradually, about ¼ c. at a time, sprinkle the flour mixture and gently but quickly fold it into the egg/sugar mixture by hand with a very clean **rubber spatula**. It is very important that the egg white structure be as intact as possible, so use your judgement with lumps. Hopefully there won't be any, but it would be better to leave a few small ones than to beat down the cellular framework you have just created.

✳ Fill the **tube pan** with the batter and quickly go around through the middle of it with the spatula to deflate any air pockets.

✳ Bake 45 minutes.

✳ Remove and immediately invert the whole pan so that the cake can cool and set hanging upside down for one and a half hours. In the off chance that this actually has risen above the top edge of the pan, set the tube up on a funnel or empty bottle. (I like to do this anyway because I think it helps to create more air flow during the cooling/setting process.)

Cutting an angel food or sponge cake is different than any other cake. You can use the special long-tined cake cutter, or divider, if you have it, but it is just as easy to use two dinner forks. With their tines back-to-back, gently insert them vertically and pull them apart little by little. Even though we had the divider and I thought it was neat to see it in action, as a kid, I still loved to make the forks work.

*Chocolate Chip Pumpkin Cookies.*

## Chocolate Chip Pumpkin Cookies
(Dairy-free, contains egg)

My kids love these incredibly soft and slightly chewy cookies and they are quick to make as long as you've taken the butter and egg out beforehand.

✴ Preheat oven to 375°.

Ingredients:
2 c. gluten-free flour of your choice
1 t. cinnamon
½ t. ground ginger
½ t. nutmeg
1 t. baking soda

1 stick (½ c.) dairy-free butter, softened (at room temperature)
1 c. dark brown sugar, pressed firmly down into the measuring cup as you fill it
1 egg
1 c. canned pumpkin
1 ½ t. vanilla extract
pinch of salt

½ bag of semi-sweet or dark dairy-free chocolate chips

✴ In a **medium bowl**, combine dry ingredients with a **whisk** or **sifter**.
✴ In a **larger bowl**, cream the butter with a **wooden spoon** or **bamboo spatula**.
✴ Mix in the brown sugar, egg, pumpkin, vanilla, and salt.
✴ When all that is smooth, mix in the dry ingredients and then the chocolate morsels.
✴ Drop plump tablespoonfuls onto **parchment** on your **cookie sheet**.
✴ Bake 12–14 minutes and enjoy!

*Almond Cake with DF "Butter Cream" Icing.*

## Almond Cake
(Dairy-free, rice-free, contains egg)

This recipe fits one **half-sheet pan** (actual inner measurement is about 11 ¾"×16 ½") or three **8" round pans**.

Having made this many times, I have found that it must be a thin cake so that it does not fall. The half-sheet is fantastic for cutting it up to make petit fours or a rectangular layered cake. (with some sort of filling…hm? I am still trying to perfect a sort of custard using all the egg yolks separated from the whites. This is hard to do without dairy milk.) Or you can just make it a frosted three-layered circular cake or just cut them separately to serve lots of people a little cake with, for instance, sweetened strawberries and coconut whipped cream.

A really simple finishing touch could just be a dusting of confectioner's sugar and it becomes a lovely not-too-sweet sweet to have with coffee and friends. Gluten-free can surprise people!

Ingredients:
coconut oil spray

⅔ c. applesauce
¼ c. avocado oil
1 whole egg
¼ t. salt

8 egg whites at room temperature (Important: See my instructions concerning egg whites at the beginning of Angel Food Cake recipe.)
1 c. sugar
2 t. vanilla extract

2 c. almond flour
¼ c. tapioca flour
¼ c. potato starch
1 T. coconut flour
1 t. guar gum

**To prepare the pan(s):**

For the **half-sheet pan**, cut parchment paper to fit the inside of the bottom, lightly spray bottom of the pan with coconut oil, place the parchment paper in and spray it again.

For the **8" circular pans** I like to use waxed paper but I think parchment will work as well. Score the waxed paper using the bottom of the pan as a guide with the tip of your scissors. Cut out the circles to fit the bottom of the pans really well (no edges curving upward). Spray inside the pans lightly with coconut oil. Insert the waxed paper circles and then spray them again.

* Preheat oven to 375°.
* Into a **medium-large bowl** sift dry ingredients together.
* In a **small bowl** (I actually use my **Pyrex 2-cup measure**r because I can measure the applesauce right in it) mix together applesauce, avocado oil, whole egg, and salt.
* Using an **electric mixer** with a **large bowl** beat the egg whites until frothy, and then begin to add the sugar gradually. When the sugar is in add the vanilla. Beating is finished when the egg whites hold a nice stiff peak.
* Use a **soft spatula** to mix the applesauce liquid mixture into the flour mixture. Incorporate it well.
* Mix into it *half* of the egg whites. This should loosen the batter so that as you now fold in the rest of the egg whites you don't lose too much of the air you have beaten into them.
* Gently spread the batter into your pan(s) and smooth the top evenly.
* Bake at 375º for 10 minutes. Open the oven door all the way briefly and turn the temperature down to 350°. Bake 10 more minutes.
* Remove and let cool for at least ten minutes. Use a **table knife or small metal spatula** to go around the edges if they are stuck. Gently turn the circular pans over onto **racks** or **plates**, peel the paper, and then turn them back right side up onto your serving plate or another rack. It will be flexible but still be gentle as you peel the paper. The half sheet will be trickier. If you have decided to cut and layer it, do the cuts first.
* To cut, you must use a **serrated knife** with a gentle sawing motion so that you don't mash down the edges.
* If you are icing the cake it must be completely cool. Be gentle. You will love the end product.

## DF "Butter Cream" Icing

Ingredients:
⅓ c. DF butter
2 c. confectioner's sugar
2 T. DF milk of your choice
1–2 t. vanilla extract

✳ In a **medium bowl** cream the butter with a **soft spatula**. Work 1 c. of the sugar into it and then add the vanilla.

✳ Keep adding the sugar and then the milk 1 T. at a time.

✳ This should be enough to cover a 9" cake with a couple of layers. The main thing is to get the consistency right. If it is too stiff it will rip up the cake but if it is too soft it will eventually fall off the cake. Adjustments may be made by adding a little more sugar or a very small amount of milk.

For chocolate "butter cream" icing add
3–4 T. unsweetened cocoa

It is up to the cook how much chocolate is needed and the same consistency as above should be maintained.

I realize that two very similar recipes follow here that I invented independently at different times. The one immediately below has almonds whereas the second one has coconut.

## Banana Bars
### (Dairy-free, egg-free, grain-free, contains almonds)

✳ Preheat oven to 350°.

coconut oil spray
⅓ c. dairy-free butter, softened
½ c. organic sugar (actually a little rounded—more)
¼ t. sea salt
3 over-ripe bananas
1 t. double-strength vanilla extract (more if regular strength is used)
½ t. almond extract

1½ c. almond meal or almond flour

¼ c. arrowroot starch

1 t. baking powder

1 pkg. mini dairy-free chocolate chips/morsels

(Once I used 1½ pkgs. of the mini chocolate chips and it was a chocolaty heaven!)

✳ Spray a **9"×13" baking dish** with coconut spray.

✳ In a **medium-small bowl** whisk together almond meal, arrowroot, and baking powder.

✳ In a **medium-large bowl** cream the butter with a **wooden spoon** or **spatula**.

✳ Add the sugar and salt and mix until well incorporated.

✳ Add the bananas, vanilla and almond extract and then the dry mixture.

✳ When the batter is well mixed add the mini morsels.

✳ Drop evenly in large spoonfuls the dough across the bottom of the pan. Gently mold and spread the dough to cover the bottom, the idea being not to drag it across the coconut oil so that it stays in place—just until it is even, no need to actually reach every part to the edges.

✳ Bake for about 27–30 minutes. The edges should be browned.

### Chocolate-Chip Banana Squares
(Grain-free, dairy-free, nut-free, egg-free)

Overripe bananas—seriously black bananas—add natural sugar and oil to this treat. You may, of course, use fresher ripe bananas. This is a rich dessert square that's amazingly allergen-free.

✳ Preheat oven to 350°.

✳ Grease a **9"×13" baking dish** with:

  1 t. coconut oil or coconut spray

✳ In a **medium bowl**, sift together:

  1½ c. coconut flour

  ¼ c. arrowroot flour

  ¼ c. tapioca flour

  1 t. xanthan gum or guar gum

  ¼ t. salt

  1½ t. baking powder

✳ In a **large bowl**, cut and mash the bananas (you have the option to remove some pieces of the dark strings if they bother you) to make:

  2 c. very ripe banana pulp (about 4 bananas)

✳ Add:
    slightly more than ½ c. sugar
    2 t. double strength vanilla
    ½ c. almond milk
✳ Combine dry and wet ingredients and add:
    1—1½ c. dairy-free chocolate chips
✳ Spoon the dough into all quadrants of the baking dish and gently press it into the dish without moving it too much so as to leave the oil in place. I always use my fingertips as if I am molding clay, smoothing the top and neatening the edges. Sometimes you have to work a little to keep the chips down in the batter as they want to separate themselves… you'll see what I mean.
✳ Bake 30 minutes (just the edge will begin to brown when it is done).
✳ Wait for it to cool completely before cutting into squares.

Note: Coconut flour can be compacted, and as a result have lumps. When this is so, I like to sift and refill the whole package so that I don't have to do so much work each time I use it.

*Blueberry Cake.*

## Blueberry Cake
(Gluten-free, dairy-free, rice-free)

I am so happy to be able to make something that tastes just like one of my favorite treats that my mom always made: her blueberry cake. The childhood memory of the flavor and having watched how she made this simple delicacy was my guide. The secret is lemon! Lemon zest and lemon juice are what make my blueberry jam pop, and they are also the key to this incredibly delicious cake.

I, like my mother, had always prided myself in the fact that I only made cakes from scratch… until we made the change in our diet. I do not have the same disdain for gluten-free cake mixes as I did for those that contain gluten, rather, an appreciation for the mixes crafted for gluten-free, dairy-free, and even egg-free cakes. I can trust the professionals on this and surrender this difficult job to them!

So when you can again have some non-gluten grains or legumes and some sugar, I think it is okay to check out a cake mix once in a while. We have tried lots of cakes which almost all have rice as a main ingredient. For this recipe I use Bob's Red Mill Vanilla Cake Mix. This is one of the few mixes that I can find that does not contain rice. It is made from potato starch, tapioca, and sorghum flours and tastes delicious.

Although this is an incredibly easy summer recipe with fresh local blueberries, you can make it any time with frozen blueberries as long as you thaw them in a strainer to let any excess water/juice drain off before proceeding with the following:

* Preheat oven to 325°.
* Spray a **9"×13" baking dish** with coconut oil—you can spread the kind in a jar just as easily but I prefer the convenience.

1½–2 c. blueberries
zest of one whole lemon
juice of half a lemon
⅓ c. organic sugar

* Mix together ingredients just above. Set aside. (This first step can also be done in advance and be placed in the refrigerator until use.)

1 package Bob's Red Mill Vanilla Cake Mix
3 eggs
½ c. melted DF butter or oil (I like avocado oil)
½ c. water
Demerara/turbinado or plain granulated organic sugar (optional)

✳ In a **medium-large bowl**, mix the cake together as per the instructions on the package. (I actually never get the beaters out for this and do it my own way—by hand. I dump the cake mix in the bowl, **whisk** the wet ingredients in a **smaller bowl** and then add that to the mix and incorporate.)
✳ With a **soft spatula** gently toss the blueberries in their syrup and then fold half of them into the cake batter.
✳ Pour and gently spread the batter in the baking dish.
✳ Bake for about 12 minutes and remove from the oven. Quickly scatter the rest of the blueberries across the top, dotting with remaining syrup.
✳ Sprinkle with Demerara/turbinado or plain organic sugar (optional).
✳ Bake it 21 more minutes. The edges and a bit on the top should be starting to brown a little, but always test your cake with a **wooden pick or skewer**. If batter sticks to it, it is not quite done.

### Pumpkin or Squash Puddings

To prepare a fresh pumpkin or squash:

It is best to begin this the night before you would like to use the fresh pumpkin or squash in any recipe.

✳ Cut the pumpkin in half. A **large knife** along with a **mallet** or the backside of a **hatchet** are useful. (However, you should not hit metal against metal, so it is advisable to have a small piece of wood between the knife blade and the hatchet.) Cut with deliberate control, never hacking. This step is the most difficult in the process because it is a very hard fruit. If you do not possess the tools or the strength, you can ask someone in the produce department to cut it in half for you in the store. However, the best choices of pumpkin and squash are usually found at farm markets and orchard outlets which may not be prepared to cut it for you. You can do it!

You may think that this is more trouble than buying the winter squash or butternut already cut and peeled, or the canned pumpkin, but I feel that once you have done this a couple of times, you will know that this is the better way. For one thing, you have your own choice of the many autumn fruits available and for another thing, there is time to do something else in the kitchen while it bakes. Also, I feel that butternut, pumpkin, turbin, and winter squashes taste much better and sweeter than the smaller squashes like acorn and delicata. Many recipes for these small tasteless wonders include a lot of brown sugar, or honey to make them palatable.

❋ Set the oven temperature to 350º.
❋ Place one or both halves (depending on the size of the pumpkin) cut side down in a shallow **baking dish or cookie sheet with inch-high edges**. Bake can be from 45 minutes to over an hour—until a fork can be poked easily through the skin into the flesh of the pumpkin. If you do this at night, you can let it cool as is overnight and then refrigerate it in the morning.

A cooked pumpkin will keep in your refrigerator for up to a week.

❋ With a **spoon**, remove the seeds and stringy fibers and then to scrape the flesh from the skin. At this point, you can make my *dairy-free pumpkin pudding* recipe in which case the extra water is beneficial to the recipe. If you want to make the *traditional pudding* recipe, which contains milk and cream, you will want to remove some of the moisture from the pumpkin meat as follows:
❋ Wet and squeeze out a clean **dishtowel**. (Rinse it under the faucet to remove any detergent residue.) With some good **string** tie the dish towel across the top of a **tall pot or pitcher** so that there is a hollow into which you will place the pumpkin meat. Let it drain overnight in the refrigerator (or outside if it is cold but not freezing).

*Ramekins with Pumpkin Pudding.*

## Pumpkin Pudding
(Contains milk and egg)

Pumpkin is "traditional" but a winter squash is what my mother always uses. They are pretty interchangeable.

* Preheat oven to 350°.
* In a **food processor** place:
    2½ c. pumpkin, cooked and drained (or canned pumpkin)
    ¾ c. evaporated milk
    ½ c. dark brown sugar, pressed firmly down into the measuring cup as you fill it
    ¼ c. organic sugar
    ¾–1 t. cinnamon
    ½–¾ t. ground ginger
    ¼ t. ground clove
    ¼ t. freshly grated nutmeg
    1 t. double strength vanilla (a little more if using regular strength vanilla)
    ¼ t. sea salt

* Process until this mixture is a smooth consistency.
* In a **large bowl** combine:
    4 large eggs, slightly beaten
    ¾ c. heavy cream
* Add processed ingredients and combine well.
* Pour the pudding into about a **2-quart baking dish**—just make sure you have at least 2 inches of headroom. If you have more pudding you can put that into some **small ramekins** or Pyrex—these will take a little less time to cook.
* Bake for about an hour. Check the pudding with a toothpick. If it comes out clean (not coated with the pudding) it is done.

It can be eaten cold but I think it is best served warm with a little plain cream or whipped cream.

Refrigerate to keep.

## Dairy-Free Pumpkin Pudding OR Egg-Free Pumpkin Mousse

This contains egg, but as explained below, it can be a dessert with no egg.

* Preheat oven to 350° (for pudding only).
* In a **food processor**, place:

2¼ c. pumpkin, cooked and drained (or canned pumpkin)
1 c. soymilk
½ c. dark brown sugar
<¼ c. organic sugar
¾ t. cinnamon
¾ t. ground ginger
<¼ t. clove
¼ t. nutmeg
1 t. double strength vanilla (a little more if you have regular vanilla)
<¼ t. sea salt
½ c. dairy-free ricotta cheese or dairy-free sour cream

* Process until this mixture is a smooth consistency.

AT THIS POINT you have made this dessert EGG-FREE. It does NOT need to be COOKED but instead CHILLED unless you are eating it immediately. It is like a pumpkin mousse.

Back to the pudding…

* In a **large bowl** slightly beat:
   3–4 large eggs
* Add processed ingredients and combine well.
* Pour the pudding into about a **2-quart baking dish**—make sure that you have at least 1 ½ inches of headroom.
* Bake for about an hour. Check the pudding with a toothpick. If it comes out clean (not coated with pudding) it is done.

Eat warm or cold. In lieu of whipped cream we have found that the whipped coconut or soy toppings in the refrigerator and freezer sections at the grocery store are surprisingly delicious.

## Quick Almond Olive Oil Cake
(Contains egg)

This is amazing because it only takes 50 minutes in total to make.

Ingredients:
5 eggs, preferably room temperature
½ t. salt
coconut oil spray or other oil spray
1 orange, not too big
¾ c. (or less) sugar
1 t. vanilla extract
1 t. almond extract
6 T. EVOO
2 c. almond flour
¼ c. (or more) sliced almonds

* Cut **parchment paper** to fit the bottom of a **9" spring form pan** or a **9" cake pan**.
* Spray the pan with coconut oil spray, insert the paper and then spray lightly again.
* Set oven temperature to 350°.
* **Grate** or zest the whole orange peel (not pith—the white part) into a **small dish**.
* Juice the orange into a **small bowl**.
* Separate the eggs, the whites into a **medium bowl**, and the yolks into a **medium-large bowl**.
* **Whisk** the yolks and add in the sugar. Mix it well.
* Add orange peel, extracts, and EVOO. After it is well mixed add the orange juice.
* Mix until it is smooth and then add the almond flour.
* With an **electric beater** or a *clean* hand **whisk** whip the whites with the salt until stiff.
* With a **soft spatula** fold in the egg whites, incorporating them well while trying not to beat the batter down too much.
* Spread the batter in the pan and sprinkle with sliced almonds.
* Bake 30–33 minutes.
* Let it cool completely before removing from the pan.

*Almond Thumbprint Cookies with my own black raspberry and sour cherry jams and mandarin marmalade.*

## Almond Thumbprint Cookies
(Contains egg)

Ingredients:
1¾ c. almond flour
1 T. coconut flour
½ t. baking powder
½ c. DF butter (1 stick) softened
½ c. sugar
1 egg yolk
1 t. almond extract
one or more good jams such as raspberry, blackberry, cherry, or apricot

* Preheat oven to 325°.
* Line a **baking pan** with **parchment.**
* In a **medium bowl** combine almond flour, coconut flour and baking powder
* In a **large bowl** cream the butter with a **wooden spoon** and then add the sugar. Mix well.
* Add and beat well the egg yolk and the almond extract and beat it until it is smooth.
* Add the flour mixture and combine well.
* Make each cookie by forming a teaspoon sized ball, mashing it slightly onto the baking pan until it is ½" high and making a hollow in the center with your fingertip, not too deeply.
* Fill each cookie with just ½ t. of desired jam(s).
* Bake 12–14 minutes until they just begin to brown at the edges.
* Do not disturb them until they are almost completely cooled.

I brought these to a Christmas party with my own jams in them and they were almost all eaten by the same person! Very gratifying!

## Blueberry Pie

1 GF pie shell (can be found in freezer section)
4 c. blueberries
zest of ½ a lemon
2 T. lemon juice
¾ c. sugar

¼ t. salt
2 T. quick cooking tapioca
Demerara/turbinado sugar (optional)

✳ Preheat oven to 450°.
✳ Mix all ingredients in a **medium bowl** and fill the pie shell.
✳ Make a paper dam—about 2-inch strip of **parchment** tucked in around the edge so the blueberry filling does not boil up and fall over the edge.
✳ Bake ten minutes at 450°, turn the oven down to 350°, and bake it 45 minute more.
✳ Remove from the oven and sprinkle with Demerara/turbinado sugar (optional)
✳ Gently remove the paper.

Let cool before serving.

# Bibliography

Davis, William, *Lose the Wheat, Lose the Weight!*, Rodale, Inc. c 2012.

Fasano, Alessio, with Flaherty, Susie, *Gluten Freedom*, Wiley General Trade, an imprint of Turner Publishing Company, New York, c 2014.

Gundry, Steven R., *Dr. Gundry's Diet Evolution*, Harmony Books, an imprint of Crown Publishing Group, a division of Random House LLC, a Penguin Random House Company, New York, c 2008.

Hagman, Bette, *The Gluten-free Gourmet: Living Well Without the Wheat*, Revised Edition, Henry Holt and Company, LLC, New York, 2000.

Peppard, Jacqueline, *New Era Healthy Eating Cookbook*, New Era Healthy Eating, Auburn, CA, c 2017.

Perlmutter, David, *Grain Brain*, Little, Brown and Company, Hachette Book Company, New York, c 2013.

Rignola, Joe, *The Definitive Way to go Gluten Free*, by Joe Rignola, Wellness Punks Health and Nutrition, c 2012.

Rombauer, Irma S. and Becker, Marion Rombauer, *Joy of Cooking*, Bobbs-Merrill Company, Inc., a subsidiary of Macmillan, Inc. New York, c 1986.

Ryrie Study Bible New International Version, Ryrie, Charles, Caldwell, Moody Publishers, Chicago, c 1994.

## Articles and Studies

Blaylock, Russell L. "Foods that Harm, Foods that Heal," The Blaylock Wellness Report, Vol. 14 No. 1, Jan 2017, Newsmax Media, Inc.

Carmen, Judy, "Is GM Food Safe to Eat?" Hindmarsh, R, Lawerce, G. editors, Recoding Nature Critical Perspectives on Genetic Engineering, Sydney, UNSW Press, 2004, P. 82–93.

Hadjivassiliou, Marios, The Lancet Neurology, UK, Mar. 2010.

O'Bryan, Tom, iTeleseminar.com/76603494

O'Bryan, Tom, "The Gluten Conundrum," seminar given at Paoli Hospital, Paoli, PA, April 27, 2012.

Smith, Jeffrey, "Are Genetically Modified Foods a Gut-Wrenching Combination?" http://responsibletechnology.org/glutenintroduction, Nov. 20, 2013.

# Praise for *The Joy of Gluten-Free* by Amanda Silver

As a doctor that recommends gluten-free diets for patients suffering from tough neurological and autoimmune based conditions I am so thrilled this book exists! It's a great resource for my patients starting a gluten-free diet. Amanda's passion is clear in her book that provides people with inspiration, clear objectives, practical solutions and encouragement.

—Dr. Joseph Childs
chiropractic neurologist, Active Integrated Medical Center

In this era of quick-fix diet books and gluten-free guides, it's rare to find a book that is both a practical resource and individual in its approach, with personal stories and tested recipes. Organized into short, easy-to-read chapters, the book is based on the latest research concerning whole-body healthcare and achieving emotional well-being. In short, the author delivers on her promise to give practical information *and* encouragement that will show you the way to long-term solutions.

—Catherine C. Quillman
food writer and former restaurant reviewer for the *Philadelphia Inquirer.*

Amanda's writing shows the true beauty of what it means to love and care for family. Also the dedication to find the right path for one's family. A mother's love is boundless. This is also true with one's relationship with Jesus. He has guided her and drawn on her creativity to provide for her family and ultimately to share with everyone. Her gift to everyone is from deep inside her heart, a heart that knows Jesus.

—Peter Fontaine
executive chef, Greenville Country Club, culinary teacher

Amanda Silver is passionately involved with her practical, informative and delicious guide to discovering new health and vitality through delicious, easy to prepare gluten-free recipes.
Amanda creates food-based remedies for common ailments and modern nutritional concerns, which make this book all the more indispensable to anyone who values good food and vibrant living. Whether you are healthy, facing medical or dietary challenges, or simply sense that you could feel better than you now do, *The Joy of Gluten-Free* has the power to transform and inspire your life.

—Francine Covelli
nutritionist, juiceologist, farm table chef

# About the Author

Having grown up with all things cooked from scratch, the author always did this with her own family. When she began developing lower-sugar handmade jams and jellies to sell in her business, she took the food safety course and has held that certificate for a decade. During this time, it was discovered that the whole family was gluten-intolerant and her lifelong interest in food and nutrition became focused in a new way. The habit of writing minutes every time she made a batch of jam trained her to always write down any adjustment made to an existing recipe or completely new one in her home cooking. The food safety knowledge was, of course, also useful at home. Combined with her concern that fewer people seem to be cooking for themselves, and her concern for the widespread suffering due to the over-consumption of convenience foods, all these things drove her to write this book.

CPSIA information can be obtained
at www.ICGtesting.com
Printed in the USA
BVHW020255150521
607436BV00010B/1974